Also by John Kilroy:

Torque
•
252 pages
•
3 books of poems
in one volume:
- Last Casino Page -
- Monkey In The Cadillac -
- I Wrench The Paradise -

Chrome Press

www.chrome-press.com

Thank you, family (Debbie, Jake, Caitlin, Matthew), for the moments of joy that I plugged into my tree like a woodpecker getting ready for winter.

Proof of Flight, first edition
Copyright © John Kilroy, 2017
All rights reserved.
Printed in the United States of America.
No part of this book may be used or reproduced in any manner whatsoever without written permission except in the case of brief quotations in critical articles and reviews.

Kilroy, John
Proof of Flight
ISBN 978-0-692-85941-4

Chrome Press
PO Box 4987
Orange, CA 92863

www.chrome-press.com

Proof

of

Flight

By

John Kilroy

How The Asphalt Can Dream You Up

Poetry In The Age Of Cinema   1

I-70   3

Lectronic Media Solstice   5

Hey! Press This Button! (Idyll)   8

Termites Eat   10

Rumbleberry Pie   12

Color Of Our Cubicles   23

Radio 30 Seconds From Now   25

Our Constant Peace Process   28

Ha!   29

Opposite Our Math Is Peace   30

Necromancer's Way With Elevators   33

Formula: Eventually, You Press Your Shoulder Against
       the Inertia of the World   36

Wakenator   37

Myths In Every Moment   39

Why Poetry Bounces Off Old Guys   42

Let's Walk The Walls   45

Essay: Reverse Rotation Engines   47

Teeth Guards At Night   50

Stripe The Beast!   56

My Unruly Bar Code Data   58

Once You've Been In Love   60

Jolly Roger Inn   61

Us The Poets Us   62

Customer   64

How To Grin Down A Bar   66

Empty Oil Barrels   68

Taco Tuesday 11:35 p.m. Promises   70

Nature Of Time In Las Vegas Airport   71

Panic Attack   72

Jimmy The Lock & Dream   74

Tropicana   75

Caldera   77

Let's Rub   79

Essay: Choice As Artifact   80

Why Spring Hurts   82

Audience   84

Geography Of Buttons   86

Essay: Synaptic Media   90

What   92

My Greatest Poems   93

The Purple Martini Glass Is A Brave Idea   95

Afloat On A Window   96

Leafspeak   108

Bloom The Flower Now   109

My Friend Hates Poetry   111

Ode To Lovers In Separate MFA Programs   113

Blow The Grey Mist   114

Excerpt I Memorized From The Rabbit Eye Stories   116

Um, Deedee Just Rose Into The Air!   117

Pull Out Your Pancreas To Speak   120

Dig It, Drill It, Cut It, Burn It...& A Poem   122

Talking Contagion Blues   124

Dark So Long We Fear The Light   125

Geometry Of Perfect   129

Mortar, Electrons, Breath & Whispers   131

Wrongly Enchanted We

Apricots   133

Pantry   135

In A Cypress Break — 1981   136

Rectangle   139

My Devil   140

Jar   141

First The Story, Then The Stars, Einstein!   142

Decorations   144

Download Me Again   145

The Peachful Life   147

Famous 2 Poems Shuffled   148

My Theory Of Chance   151

My Theory Of Time   152

Indestructo   153

Postcards From Paris   154

Beware The Body Greed   155

Origin Of Ghost Ships   157

What We're Born For   159

Apocalips   161

Honey Time   163

The Way Ray LIfts Days   165

Kernel   167

Blue   169

Unsever & See   170

One True—Never The Same For 2   171

The Stuff Of Poetry   172

Denny's—8:30 a.m., Wednesday   173

Calamity Divines Clem   175

Sons Of Erin Make Wayward Scientists   177

Egg   179

Story   180

Science Of Growing Old   182

Litterfall   184

Corsair   187

Hamlet Days   188

We'll Have The Boys Back Home By Christmas   189

My Brain Is A Bartender   190

All The Underworld (Hack The Black!)   192

Muscle   193

Dawn Of Gone   195

Croc   197

Once, I Was   199

Calling All Copters   201

Down The Hall   203

Carlotta, Mist & Rain   204

Turtle   206

Who We Are Now   208

Dylan   210

Pond   211

Ta-Pocketa   214

L.A. Apocalypse Cartoon   215

The Phantasm Quartet (And Who Are You?)   217

Flash   220

Dream of Mass   221

Small Proof There's Only One Of Me   222

Outside   223

How The Asphalt Can Dream You Up

Poetry In The Age Of Cinema

Lena got all leather for her motorbike, M. Ducati,
on his kind of night, avenger of clerks & cretins,
jewel thief because everything is stolen, champagne
sipped from a bota bag on her back, piped into her helmet,
pistol clipped to the back of one boot (this whole game
sometimes gets played that way, and she won't go dead
for being stupid). Maybe a smash and grab. She knows
the city's grid like a coroner loose in veins, alleyways
too narrow for cop cars, tunnels to confuse copters,
little storage units here and there to ditch a bike,
walk off to a nearby bar and call for a ride home.
The way she kneels before him, opens a black glove,
and a string of diamonds lays there like an answer
for everything, a pass in this world to go go go
everywhere now! Then, he'll read her a poem,
and she weeps, and holds onto him like the earth
had split right there in the Echo Park palace,
his body anchored above their abyss. Then,
they make love like a bomb squad's worst day,
and it's so quiet and careful and fevered until
she cuts the blue wire, and then they die ever
so voluptuously. She lives for her four perfect

acts each year, and he must match them, poem
for heist. And that's how they must live. Seconds
gong and the furniture shakes; their tale
available to lightning rods...Richter Scale.

I-70

Midnight tells you what a road can be,
how the asphalt can dream you up.
250 miles without incident, just out
of radar, testing if it's tough enough.
How you don't want to lead the world;
you just want to chase it. Distance
cowers down on state highway signs.
Time gets clocked on tachometers.
Run Indy into St. Louis. A capsule
afloat in crackerjacks, coffees, jerky,
Dunkin' Stix and enough Marlboros
to name a cancer ward after me.
Speed gypsy in love with I-70 West,
chance for pure hurtle, as I imagine
someone else's memories flickering
out past the breakdown lane, but, no,
it's trees, rivers, bridges, cornfields,
and worse, things WE owned, stowed,
Viet Nam and high school football,
Holy Rollers limbed to Jesus, angry
lovers as we slammed down the phone,
all that more or less harmed us all,
Speedwayland to Budweiser Town.
You gas it—248 strips down. Barely
there in a Citgo Travel Plaza, ghost
through Terre Haute, where radio dies.
Ford F-150, electron on a neural map,
pulsing free of cops. (God bless tax cuts!)
Somewhere, eastbound, a husband runs

to set up his tabletop display in Akron
by 9 a.m. He'll sell his guts out. Peace,
my friend, but she wants it both ways.
Shoulda never let her go to the race
at IRP. Nobody told you about a driver
suit? How it's a soldier's uniform
for the country of Wild-As-Hell?
How a driver looks when he pulls
his helmet off July nights? Yes!
Exactly! A lit match! Don't worry.
She knows which way the future
rides, which way the empty truck.

Lectronic Media Solstice

In my hacker's suit of netherdawn/hunter's night,
digital-invincible, for my politest crime wave,
jazzy snare drum riffing out 0s and 1s, glib,

in all this shared cranium space, rebels pout
the spiel: we must start thinking like Ferraris!
(as in, don't thank me, run me over!)

(as in, what's a passport to a nova?)
(as in, the end of white women slithering.)
Just type the clues, despite memory-filled cavity,

information neither good nor bad, in collusion
with ground sloths of the industrial age, how
we eat the moralists' eggs, bleed in facts.

(It's not wrong, but the way that we cash in.)
They hunt us in Bali, we hunt them in Jersey,
hear them from space, kill us in our office complex.

Coin or copulation, doctors chart only sales,
and leave churches to count the dead, our final war
about time, conflict of centuries, blank tech manifesto.

Be brave my little parasite, the seer crunches numbers,
go to sleep my little stash, heresy can be deceiving.
Ask the boy then ask the bishop, because God gave us

guns, born without a neighborhood, sludge shopper, lethal
cinematic love, every bedroom fetish for the boot, crawl
unto me, vile reproduction, rough trade death, moan

of crisis, no cure for patent leather hats, blame
also ticks the atomic clock, technology of coma.
They string you up with hope, "Don't worry,

tonight's thunder is on my credit card."
Same old buffalo tears, yet we still seek the toxic
as aquatic birds to marsh, each tomorrow slipped

into a vending machine, our shared recall
strictly television. We raffle off the dumb, then
the smart, until we're all hung on carnival wires,

alcohol our most effective political argument,
sleep the last land of truth, our snoring
protests so loud . . . no wait, that's us

in a scream-and-run dream, kelp color
of bones turns to albino children, alive
and drowned at once, floating, movement

strictly fashioned by prevailing current,
until tender words require condoms,
nothing more expensive than our acts,

and so we save ourselves to death,
minimalism of cows, stoic as a mall kid
alone, retail clawing away her skin,

as the new Eve covers herself in greed.
A savior merely says, "Yes, I'm advertised."
But don't destroy the phone lines, everyone agrees,

plotters in Portland sync with the FBI in Kabul,
every cell phone capable of calling in an air strike,
battle lines vaporized by the need to be a man,

calumny the name of every-night TV, coroners
star in ratings bonanzas, although no one's sure
what's dead, who's dead, life the width of shoelace.

Get drunk and call a number for promises of love,
(cheaper to cut a check for the disappearing frogs.)
What's a forest if not logs? Wander in video games,

in fear of all unpaved. De-spine the young, then pour
the children into pudding molds. Jail skate rats for grinding
miracles on the library steps and regulate each wave

for the safety of surfers, the saying of all this
my need, my reverie writhing up from a bare floor,
how I spin purpose so far, so far from our one sun.

Hey! Press This Button! (Idyll)

We caught the sun rioting off the Keys,
cut the sails, slowed the rented sloop.
Now, I've heard the world talk, but

I never heard it say, quite like this,
"We want to watch you two fuck."
I mean, isn't the world mostly about bad luck?

"Let's just sit and tan," she said,
handing me a bottle. "Oil me up."
The sun twitched a little hotter. Later, lotter.

Her fingers in bird beaks behind her back
unknotted her bikini top; her white cotton shorts
dropped soft as sighs to the teak deck.

Old pirate wails etched the summer trades,
as she got down on her hands and knees,
then stretched prone onto a stolen hotel towel,

ankles crossed. Attired in bracelets. Entirely.
Hands fast become addicted to lubricated skin.
They'll have fearful cravings for more of this!

Slide my chest up the full length of her back.
My physical center finds its God-given groove,
and I whisper, in the faith that poets have

in the power of such words, such moments,
"Spread your legs." "Aye-aye, captain,"
she says, in sleepy panther growl.

Toes pointed, ankles drift apart, slow as lake canoes,
bows tied to the same dock cleat. And there enters
a slipperiness of two from one, all from me.

Termites Eat

Morgan tapped his fingers on a jar of woman's bones.
Yes, yes, easy as termite hunger in a wooden railing
it was, as she dropped from a high porch, head hits
cement wrong, and life falls quiet. Mother's dead.
History embeds its ends. Crazy how he could kick
a field goal with her now, with the right kind of vase,
or bowl a strike, the kind of fun things they never did
because in all the constant yakking of the universe,
Mom always squawked mean as a caged parrot
someone set on fire, desperate for your attention,
hoping to fly free, wanting to bite your finger off.
"I guess, in her long speech, she said her piece,"
thought Morgan. "I don't know what she meant."
He couldn't help but think she proved Original Sin.
Yes, in time, she had thrown her sentence in. Quick.
Inarticulate. Brusque. Opposite of conversations
that somehow take flight. She spoke heavy
as a handyman who carries cans of paint
to a backyard fence only to find no need
for another coat. There were parties. Fear.
Rushing about. Morgan pumped distance
in each room she entered. Invented space.
Surprised the crack of her skull came naturally
as vacuum cleaning! Next, any hopefulness
pooled in most of us just flat ran out. She was
a woman who drank too much, complained
bitterly to her children about their lack of religion
and became a motel clerk when the waitressing
destroyed her legs, rivered blue in varicose veins.

"Mom would be on the graveyard shift tonight, if
it weren't for those damn bugs," Morgan mused.
If they were people, he'd have a lawsuit going,
maybe a criminal case. No, wait, these insects
always win, he thought. They eat everything up.
She never saw his Dodge. He kept her last note
to him, with a $50 check to spend in Vegas
on his next trip. Washed away her blood
with the garden hose, then hung it back.
Organized a funeral like buying a new car.
Tonight, he'll sneak onto the golf course,
pour her ashes in the same trap as Dad,
talk to her one more time, wait and listen
for a cancer-cured voice to declare
what's wrong with him and all of this.
Crazy joy of a buried sound. Pedal. Road.
He notices the trees don't meet overhead,
as the moon bales light onto the Intrepid.

Rumbleberry Pie

No more a poet than many. Ill
from our waste stream of words
that yak-yak me poor with thoughts,
strike me hard as homemade liquor
jolts me with the jitters, and how
many times language troubled all

I once set out to do, a stupid kid
who bought all the best meanings.
But words trick you into faith, then
get read out loud in courtrooms
until you're penniless or worse.
"Planning Retirement" closed fast

since no one knows how to age,
unlike old Bible Acts when sages
puffed tents, teepees and yurts
with raw visions bred into smoke,
and the old told the young all
about to happen, despite prayer

or love, hard work or luck. Hell,
even I who knows nothing wants
to tell you all I've tried to forget;
it rides the desolate wind of facts
aside me in full banshee tease.
The profane and the abominable

much a part of each day as noon.
You have to hide from half this life.
Anyways, I signed up in bad faith
for the creative writing course
offered in the extension program
at Cal State Fullerton, at night,

in room 422, every Wednesday,
by a professor who looked lost.
My children gone, I just needed
something to blot the spill of days.
It beats me what I hope to find,
as if another world exists I missed

those years in the purchasing dept.
To sum up my life: I paid the bills.
Zeroed it out. All debts paid. Yeh,
I'd pray for blank dates to drop and
disappear away before my payday,
as every hour awake just drains you,

and cash never arrives soon enough.
I'm the last person to ever trust
behind the wheel of an epic poem.
"La vérité est jugée par la distance."
(You don't speak this language?!)
Love is the tear gas in our cold war

of doubt. Been coughing, choking
from riot gas for 40 years, and now
I can say, "Steadfastness counts"

—our one antidote to tomb room
or fully strangered night dives. Yes,
I lack the stuff of our greatest lies,

you see, a tree is a tree. I own one.
It's nothing but trouble each fall
and it's destroying my driveway.
I've experienced this life. Alright?
Everyone I meet is mistaken, yet
some have great cars. Period.

That's meaning for you: Traction.
Mystery's bought with $100 bills.
Bluster all you want, but accept it
(best way to avoid heart disease).
Then—are you ready?—a poem
read by the prof twitterpated me!

I found I housed dimensions such
as our jimmyrigged universe! Physics
includes me! Huh? Yes! I could feel
space a thing inside! A poem torqued
it over and onto itself. No clue what
the poem meant, but I understood.

It revved my long plundered soul into
a jumping bean, or kitten and string.
You can be empty and full, Einstein!
All there is we do not know, you write
it! IT! Don't wait on broke knowledge!
You can move, just move, you know?

Let an obtuse, dark, invisible reason
stomp down on the accelerator until
rebirth detonates a student's desk
on the fourth floor of Humanities!
Teacher, my preacher, we must talk!
Tell me what this is! Give me snakes!

I'm ready to bleat it out in tongues!
We agreed to meet in Aristotle's Place
across the street over beer, chili fries,
and a fresh pack of menthol smokes.
My writing teacher would rub his eyes,
and kept cleaning his wire glasses,

not as if he wanted to see better, no,
like he didn't want to see at all, a man
who glimpsed the world one way, then
cleaned it all off his vision, expecting
life as he knew it to go away. Ornery,
groping for sun, life returns full force.

He bent and twisted his glasses to twigs,
and picked them up fearful, slow, gentle
as tiny bones of an old pet or someone
he once knew. I never saw a sadder man
rub his eyes with the heels of his hand
so hard, erasing eyesight from his head.

The plastic nub fell off one end. Help!
I sat there crazy distracted! This poet,
my sudden priest, will stab his own eyes!

Not much got explained until 3 Buds in,
and then he talked deep, as if unveiling
spine. Repositioning skin. "...you could

"trace those eyes on peacock tailfeathers,
with skin 6 tones closer to earth than mine,
legs that make you want to shoot the river.
Go back with me, please, and witness how
Falona inspects the candy 4 steps down
the jelly bean line, while I control boxes.

"Too far away to hear me sigh, too close
for me to keep my breathing measured
for the 8 hours to stare at her all day,
escape to dinner and TV and then all
control dissolves in sleep, and dreams
bring Falona right back to me, acloud,

"abird, aconvertible, asurfboard, awave,
gone is the clean room dress of day,
covered up surgeon tight, loose gown,
mouthcover, haircap. Can you imagine,
what hellish myth is this, slammed close
to a woman so stiff and grave in toxic

"shades of green, invented to disappear
us into an army of nobody we'll ever
remember, only to have her undulate
nightly in cobra attacks into my head?
So lewdly appareled I searched dream fields
for a husband, cops, or old ladies redfaced

"at these displays of lawless, wanton curves,
marauding voluptuously to brown horizons,
loud eye racket, vowing never to straighten,
never to lose their Edenic bounce. "Never!"
Draw her, and you have the map of love.
Yet, we stand as posts holding up nothing

"but a dry, brittle temple to 'do not touch.'
I stare at my boxes and tawny Falona,
little more than another factory column,
yet, because I'm a poet, I'm an auditorium!
A Grand Central Terminal! A customs hall
for all sorts of exotic people who meet

"and pass and scurry and wait. Space station.
No, a planet out there among the interstellar
trade routes, a giant rest stop on a flight
from the Andromeda Galaxy to Centaurus A.
You can walk around in me. Visit in me.
Peoplewatch in me. Hell, you can ride

"dinosaurs and jetstreams in me, while I
keep one eye on my boxes, one eye
on every man's oasis just 4 steps down,
in acrid vapors of sugar and candy dyes.
A poet is a planet loose in irregular orbit
off this ground, maybe not high enough

"for air traffic control, but in an altitude
of our own making, we will ourselves
unbound, twice past endless, big bang

enough to stare back on all we think
is here and pronounce judgments, tell
you whether it's this or that, diffuse

"all the confusion, hold your hand then
fling you from here to impossible, out
of your Payless shoes clean to stardust.
A poet is a place big enough to lose
your mind or get along fine without it.
I'm here, quiet, so densely packed

"at my post. Honest, I'm 3 cubic feet.
Yet that's space enough for a poet
to see your family for who they are,
review the future as it is, grow young
again, as the kid who stole bubblegum,
then refused to chew it out of fear

"that God commands bad kids to choke
to death on anything they love and can't
afford but find their own way to get it.
On top of all this, our company hires
a roomful of engineers somewhere
dedicated to getting rid of all of us!

"Machines don't even notice Falona;
but they keep all our boxes perfect.
Being human is our curse. Flatline
is the heartbeat engineers crave.
Nothing in my pockets now, I still
let her know this was temporary.

"A literary mag of some 36 pages
had published my poem, "Bark."
An editor said I had his very style.
Got all A's in English. Dean's List.
Pre-approved for certain success,
while Falona could care less: Home

"and husband, her Mom, sisters,
brothers were her whole world.
Her vegetable garden mattered
more than New York city news.
I gathered Falona's life all up
like flowers wait on falling pollen,

"and heard one day, during break,
"Mumble ferry I," on a cell phone
call to her giant 6'5" trucker man.
At least, that's what I thought I heard.
At a dreary Chili's Christmas Party,
I caught half a whisper in his ear,

""Humble merry lie." He released
a bank embezzler's chicane of smile
after taking in the day's big deposit.
At a picnic on the company lake,
I heard her say, "Rumbleberry pie,"
and he pushkissed her so hard

"you could hear them crash against
the wall of a frozen yogurt stand.
I have to know. I wait. Finally, I say,

"I've heard about your rumbleberry pie.
Could you bring it to the candy factory
one day, soon? I'd love to have a taste."

"She sneezed a laugh. "This is no place,
my friend, for Falona's rumbleberry pie.
Believe me. Who told you? Never mind,
rumbleberry pie is my secret. You know,
one day, my man won't see me again
as the 19-year-old girl he first met,

"but I'll still serve him up a hot mess
of rumbleberry pie every night he wants.
That's all a woman needs, the only recipe
for keeping the same man in your bed
every night for years and years. Forget
the factory. Forget the college, kid.

""You go out there and find your own
slice of homemade rumbleberry pie."
And that's where the first poetry book
comes from. 46 poems, all to prove
I was bigger than Falona's husband."
The professor ground his sore eyes

as if he could crush them into powder.
"Know this: poetry cannot save you."
He hollowed out the night. Air turned
icy, and my body temperature dropped
with every breath. Resurrected hours
earlier, transcendent, first time ever,

then defrauded by the first saint found
in this new religion, who used poetry
like I once bought big brown drinks
for reluctant women in hotel bars.
I feel a thing I can't put into words,
and poetry verifies it like a hammer

to the knee describes your nerves.
The drive home is endless, as time
appears to be as real as our word.
There's no destination up ahead.
You just put it in gear and go until
the fuel is gone. Nothing to know

in our travels. A species incapable
beyond easy food and reproduction.
This night manufactured nothing
as if nothing was what we needed
to win a world war. I had nothing
in my car pressed against the glass,

nothing outside pounding to get in.
I hate for evidence to be a decision,
for so much to be pathetic invention.
All my life, not much was ever real
if it could not weigh down my hand
until a poem sent me...can't go back.

I am no poet, house no galaxies,
but maybe I have buildings. Empty
theater? I know a poem lights it!

Have faith, friends, poetry is sonar,
an internal organ, an atom smasher
where energy bursts into matter!

I started to rub my eyes, and felt
the betrayal of this act. Not for me.
I'll see this world for 10,000 years!
I have to believe a poet one day
will pull back his head, face to face
with sky, open his mouth, roar out

a beam of light back at the sun.
Hey! I just welcomed Union Station
into my rib cage! It's now waiting
on its first train. Whoever you are,
wherever you may rest, express
route a starliner this way, west.

Color Of Our Cubicles

Fontarino's hair shouted shiny black hallelujah's up
to the office ceiling, weakly tiled in offed winter days.
"You got your department budget done? It's Tuesday."
Carol fought the mirror back into the drawer—disbelief
on the line, her new reflection unruly as a flopping fish.
Man, how cinematic the world gets as it crumbles down
our own dark well, in shattering German ceramic or
carbon fiber on a race car. Fingernails grind pit walls
of sienna soil, tree roots, rock, as we fall. The vast
hard surface beneath our feet abandons us so fast
in a gravity of emptiness! God, all the cement, wood
and asphalt we somehow swallow. "Please give me
until 5 p.m." Puddle-voiced. Crumpled. He sensed it.
But all pockets long emptied for the job, he just nodded,
and accepted the good side of Carol's face as a way out.
What was Fontarino to do? Weep now, and vow revenge?
"Cool," he said. Office somewhere in a robot's intestines.
She ate a mint, spread budget sheets dense as war maps.
Ledgers and numbers must learn the smack of tears.
She married one man for his laughable dreams, a painter,
then finally fucked a man for power NOW with money.
No real muscle to her husband until last night, funny,
when he found a right cross. Her lawyer cared less.
His famine sex is food line time and grab—"Mine!"
The trick is to get out and disappear, taxi tender.
Her lover calculates everything, moral as needs be,
taking depositions now coolly among the parapets,
while she broadcasts bruises throughout the work day.
He's respected mostly for perfect flight. "He's quick."

And what was it, touching cheekbone, reminded her
of the Flacken boy, dead this week in war, because oil
is what we do. Fuel is who we are. Random rocket fire
into the Green Zone in hopes of killing any American
who believe with their bodies in pre-emptive strikes,
CIA evidence, redneck empire, yahoo war, petroleum.
"It's just hard to imagine that brick-haired boy dead,"
her mother said as the news entered her throat, shot
back out again in our old friend disbelief. Imagine
street hockey kids destined for mortar shells,
the same way they tore up headlands for homes,
all the green hills and red hair churned to death
by the same sweeping roundhouse clocked Carol.
We'll never understand the fight ring we're living in.
The score! The score! Find a corner! Check the score!
Right. Why all office walls are painted the color of fog,
because absence gives the sobbing beast a sense of space.
We leave our cubicle unmarred each day by our one story.

Radio 30 Seconds From Now

Elevate where you're at,
no gravity for action, no
hard Earth-bound limit
to a kiss. Hell, zoom
past orbit! Fealty only
to what we all could be
in just 30 seconds time.
Let's see...

Cowboy and a miner....
They talk about the sun.
More of the story later.
(We write time.)

Take the word 'love.'
Now put dollar signs to it
as they do, but knowing
it's not the same as touch.
(We write distance.)

Just as a wind arrives
a limo outside the office
some days to haul you
far into the forest. Smells
of minerals and old water,
as all that's dead refuses
to be swept away, discarded,
and living is all the brighter
for it. As the shock of daylight

at funerals—impossible
for some of us to mourn
long. (We right death.)

My one problem? I don't feel like accepting a chain of
humanity where I add a sentence to the book of
awareness, die, then a reader picks it up and adds the next
sentence. That's how insects do things. Me? I want to
know it all right now, and then say it in such a way it's the
Pyramids...the Grand Canyon...the Great Wall of China
...the big, knowable thing that we might finally discover in
30 more seconds, then make it visible from outer space.

Be the amplification
speaker for whatever
is wired through the soil
into our bare soles,
as I wait quietly
somewhere of so little value
there's no fence around it.
Imagine!

Still with me? Well,
the cowboy told how
he's got skin cancer
now, but he still calls
cattle home at night,
with church organ lungs.
The miner coughed some
more, some more, some more,
some more. Ain't it funny, two men,

one dying from our great god sun,
one dying from the dust you must
dig to find. You get a chance
to know there's no way to win.

But a world of stabbing lights!
Like the day that red bike
was born to me, beneath
a hooker Christmas tree.
I'm sure I forgot to breathe.
No childbirth ever that way!

Think of one thing you'd like to keep
even if you're offered eternal life
without pain to hand it over....
what are you holding onto?

As if nothing scared us as children.

And ocean waves had their own source of light!
(Poets lie to get to the truth of things
because scientists refuse to teach
what they haven't proved, leaving
almost everything entirely mine!)

And here comes the law I enacted today:
Hunt your future like something you'll eat
so tantalizingly 30 seconds from now.

Our Constant Peace Process

Johnny Manta Ray dealt with death
same as any business anywhere:
slip Tone some eels, pat him on the back,
watch Donatello's Lincoln blown to hell.
Georgia sighed, "Evil sure gets pretty,"
her dress sequined in happy thoughts,
and it hung absolutely right. After all,
what's not wonderful about sparks
in the night, homemade stars, the nearer
and the now? "I don't want trouble any more,
and when you have a problem with something,
cut off the head. That's what Jesus said."
"No, boss, I don't think Jesus said that."
"Somewhere in the Bible. I'm no reader,
but this is as right now as 10,000 years ago."
Georgia explained to Tone how she was young,
and needed money, not so smart, weak,
how it ain't wrong if, "I hadda, hadda, hadda..."
"Porn ain't so bad," said Tone, "But Johnny feels
the news is up to him. Donatello's mistake
is employee-related. He shoulda just kept quiet."
"Let's talk about something else. Murder weighs
a ton. Georgia, tell Tone about my 'Volare'
the night I crooned out all those clouds."

Ha!

Mister, you could tie my arms to separate horses,
shoot your gun and holler "Ha!" and I believe
you could pull me straight apart and a fortune
would be all that's left, foretelling a future,
or maybe it'd be a wish that poltergeists
around then shimmers fine away....

...some mystery life itself gave me knowledge to say...
I mean, you can talk about cars and auto parts stores
and how shopping malls grab and grab and grab,
all the internal combustion engine noise out our windows,
how some people buy jet plane tickets and go to France
while other people are just itching to chop someone's head off,
and how there's news but it don't seem like news...more
like internal combustion engine noise, a noise we suffer through,
a noise we can't do anything about, there whether or not
we push the on button, like my own ears aren't what it's all about,
...I mean, there's all this stuff, and it feels like the walls of a well,
and there's daylight and lightbulbs but when it comes time
for me to say what I want to say, I've got to holler
from a darkness, holler to a light that I think I made up.

I know full well now I'm going to die
and I never meant a thing,
but I like to think there's an invisible snake inside
that's been feeding off of me, off all I wanted
when I wanted what was right,
and this snake is big—
not angry, not a killer, just big—

and the minute I die, it slithers out of me.

What I try to holler
is where the snake goes.

Opposite Our Math Is Peace

Shock, yes, if tears were suddenly to turn, and fall up,
where we'd watch them shoot back through the clouds
to find every sunny day lost to this sad reverse of rain,
but our experience is so small a plot that such surprise
seems merely fencepost and wire, first bump of beyond,
as the volume would ring no great GONG, accustomed
to (example) war follows war, as we are. Blood on TV

is a sofa in the living room. Math purity! Locust love!
Peace? Not on your life! Might as well make a Caddy
fly as untick and distock this clock! Much like genius
in plane design, new alloys, composites, aero...only
brings more of what we expect. Manufacture & devour!
Create & destroy! Expand loss! A warm-hearted hug?
Don't make me laugh. Free, yes, and you can't ever

get enough, but no one can sell it, so it's not the stuff
of good employ, as we must step in order each stone
we see stretched across a creek, and can't imagine
a busboy who refuses to be a waiter. Each morning,
we open the door to the same old front porch. Yes,
yes. It's still there. Jeez. The old shrubbery waits
to be trimmed with the latest axe when it's on sale.

Purchasing is now the primordial soup. Ooze out!
Rebirth yourself outside the lines we've mapped
with fear, lust, $$$, years, you surveyors peering
deep into a television set—loop of training films.
And how revealed truth appears to us a mistake,
a thing to ridicule. As if we'll acknowledge wizards
when they're 12 inches in the air, not 10. Forget

years of discipline and abandon, just wait for
the laughter to die (Shapeshifting's the thing,
stoopid, not the thing!) Sure. Ignore this poem.
Or use it to tilt the world off its axis. Ha! You see?
Extravagance is to be loved and adored, naturally,
in the monsoon season I bring to this page. Or,
well, I'm just another mailman delivering the junk

new facts, with tired, sore, mass-produced feet,
like naming state capitals, or never having argued
against the tide barging into the shore because
no one else ever has. See this as a garage to be
cleaned Saturday afternoon. Maybe a previous
tenant left a toy under the workbench...diaries...
love letters...art once held on refrigerator doors...

Unearth wonder! Balloons and fireworks lie buried,
or in those eyes haunting the cubicle next door.
Be curious now!? Then, demand the world be
set right, as if the homeless know what they do,
the worst ruined with mouths gnarled, gone gargoyle.
Truth remains to be spit out like a choke of phlegm,
as in our physics of light and consciousness, so

a drowning man sees himself in a film screened
into the seaweed, and we cannot distinguish
between knowledge and death, more aware
we will soon be gone, in our brief Constitution
for the Martyrdom. Live life as if you chose to,
and accepted death as a penalty fee. We vote
with blood, and better yet, lifetimes. I, too, can't.

But, thank you for hoping it could be possible,
as we all cancel all our applications nightly
to download and upload so we are joined
in any event. We maybe get a glimpse,
Savior? Not one of us. Sure we could watch
a coal-black stallion turn to glass as it charged into
an airport, and all the milling merchant commuters

will still make their flights. Our greatest need, amoeba-
like, impossible to not be where people are. We breathe
company, fish that cannot swim away from Lake DNA.
Dear reader, you are safe here because gravity works.
I won't leave you, and that's how poems get buried.
I knew who I was when I had a future; but a past
disintegrates ideas of extravagant function, shock

of finding we'll kill the prototypist with everything
we do. What all was destroyed by fork? And who
all have died so that I might use this ignition key?
We flagellate propulsion with 12 billion feet and stop
at walls to argue and fight and spraypaint names
until one of us says, "There is no wall. Watch me."
Poets serve as traffic cops at mirrors on the mist.

Necromancer's Way With Elevators

I will die a brand new death. Do my weeping
in a perfect state of health. Our best goodbye
comes sure of all we've got to lose. Next,
when I'm ever whom I ever was, I'll build
something out of stone. Alone. Feel the weight
of this life, witness a thing close to permanence—
clumsy and rude—as I am likely to ever come.
Having done all that, in some years time, I will
jet ski down the River Styx, the day I die, wave
and yell, "I'm here!" over the sound of blasted
water, happy enough, having left an odd stack
of rocks. You see, my history is rearranging air.
Turn feral ideas into runway models, put truth
where people stare. Only to learn readers pray
for death. Yes! Step One to get reborn! As what?

Nothing that takes guts. Years. Or action, even.
As if life is merely waking more than once. Owed
a way to brave for simply having eyes, perhaps,
or made bold by all they learned in high school,
as if required reading homework left them divine.
Maybe I participated. Perhaps that was my life.
Bringing new air to the motionless, enchanting
them to believe they're on a runaway train
from Frankfurt to Berlin, or record-breaking
quarter-mile sprint, a hunt through forest dense
with ill whisperings and a taloned, fingery moss.
Every line I create might end in a righteous sort
of jail time for people with barely faith enough
to pull the tab of a beer can or aim the remote.
And so, this renewed acquaintance with death,
who has remained my spectacular old friend,
as if we once rode three-speeds down a dry
Santiago Creek bed, dared each other to enter
the hobo's lean-to, while he wandered around
our neighborhoods offering to sharpen knives.
Night, and only the necromancer believes
dawn is anything else but choice. Want. Ah,
this lust in the black arts for a lurid totality,
a world woven in joint quilt, or shared much
as a hologram, how we download the real
in sleep and it beams somehow before us,
withhold now my reflection from mirrors.
People describe my features. It isn't me.
And maybe I have but one thing to say,
a poem written in the ink of all my days,
unlike the journalist who types a period

after river otters will go extinct if
nothing is done, lights a cigarette,
and cracks wise on the mayor's wife.
That's it? That's how we are? Picnickers
by the Johnstown flood? "Look, there goes
the Williams house! There's the church!"
Yet, a poem exists as opposed to a gun.
That's what I'm saying. Plus, I love
the way Mr. Death never quits. Reader,
you're safe. Take the pill. Get surgery.
Rest. You're the one who'll never die.
I'm laughing. I feel sheepish. Alright,
I'll take the chance of a poem, versus
granite, stupid to the end, wrong
until the Glen Canyon dam's gone again.
While the TV shouts out floor numbers
in a skyscraper mortared by agreement,
I demand elevators loosed among the clouds,
my own death as relentless role model.

Formula: Eventually, You Press Your Shoulder Against the Inertia of the World

Chet ate lunch at his desk one day.
+
He read over population figures
+
For a year in which he would be gone.
+
He penciled out some easy math.
+
Twice the wars? Double the famine?
+
"I'm glad I'm dead," he said,
+
Drinking diet pop, eating veggie burgers.
+
Editor of the company newsletter,
+
He wondered about the new health benefits meeting announcement
+
Because Chet wanted a packed house.
+
"Ah, hell," he thought.
+
"Finish your lunch before you worry about that."

Wakenator

I've been a man for which there are tools
wrenched him into working harder, more time
away from family, drunk with clients until
he's putting the price of a recent DUI
on a company expense report. That's me,
as if I saw the tools first as a child then
cupped body parts, or strapped arms or
legs or fingers into immobility, scarred up
my mouth, distorted my eyes with sticks
so that one day I'd be a man that fit
the machine. My strategy succeeded
until I could no longer dream. A big help
in keeping myself alone and streamlined
to get the job done, to take things away,
accumulate, get a ski boat and a beer
on a July afternoon, with a woman yelling,
"Hit it," and I accelerate over water
faster than any squall or lake bird.
Then, God hurricaned Ponchartrain.
I did OK, but the house got bruised
bad, like it had been in a fight, electricity
gone right away, no real news for days,
and when I went to check on Wakenator
in the storage yard 10 miles south,
there was nothing but orphan homes,
unmoored, crashed, pale, dead.
When I drove to the grocery store
to post a picture of my boat in case
anybody saw it somewhere, the wall

was covered in people's faces, xeroxed
photos of folks, disappeared by water
or the chaos, paper flapping away,
concrete sprouting 100 frantic wings.
So much gone it looked like prophecy.
I'm damaged much as I ever wanted:
I know it's guys like me hold the lever
and the key. I did this. Not the rain.
Not the levee. Just the cogs I ride.
And so, I found what I was fitted for.
Perdition. Gears grinding perdition
until we can only guess at the number
of corpses. I've got to pry my way out.
Find someone in the wild. Mimic human.

Myths In Every Moment

I.
It ran like a trip wire taut and thin
across Corinne's gunked-out teeth,
secret that sent her blanking up against
walls, keeping her mouth well guarded.
But, young women can't disappear
quick as an exclamation point shrinks
down into a dot! So, she flutter-smiled,
as her lips uncurtained silver surprise
when you made her laugh, worried
her braces somehow signaled attack.
"Wires are for batteries," she'd say
to her dog Brandy, then hoped again
Astarte might one day rule the world.

II.
In the manner of dust, dirt vague now
in the sky wiping the blue off the plains,
broke loose into town, a hesitant sort
of brown, the terra severed from solid,
roamed like banished shadows refusing
to be underlings to all the life it gave.
"Bad times when that's what you see
at your bustop...the last of the topsoil,"
thought Chris. In the manner of youth,
unchained from crops, you catch a ride
with the wind, join up with your friends,
and if you want to, you blow this valley
back to desert once again. He's less

than one year on the job, first one out
of college, and he stands wondering
what did the dirt decide today? How
goes the howling of farmland? What
does a lunar surface, exactly, look like?
Well, son, nothing lasts long in employ,
not even the ground beneath your feet.
We turned everything to zoo rules,
a planet based on refrigerator units
for polar bears. Still, some teenagers
watch dust clouds eager as hunting dogs,
like traffic to the party tonight. Yes!
Unruly up that old horizon! Chaos always
looks like a good place to hide. We never
wanted to be farmers. Sure, it was cash
in the bank, a way out of hunger. But
we can't build a church that bans our DNA!
Hell! For Chris, It's just another 7:09. Waiting
on the 7:07 to jump a downtown Indy bus
from Clermont, his head pointed East,
hoping for his ride to show before earth
arrives to enter every orifice, loose upon
a wind, demonic airborne herd of harpies.

III.
Madeleine can't locate the mute button
for the TV news shooting at her from the gas pump.
The apparent facts today make her feel bad for being
a mother, unable to name the god that doomed us
to die from all our hunger...how we'll eat everything.
Her Lycanthrope Yoga revealed the one story

that cannot be told in fear that it's all too true.
"I'm just going to go," she thought, always alert
to bad voodoo mucking up odd parts of her day,
faith long gone for the god of frontier that allowed
us all to leave and leave and leave until we took
his kingdom, now there's no place left to go.
No gas.
No TV news.
We'll see how far she gets.
We who believe Coyote won't truly win.

Why Poetry Bounces Off Old Guys [To Be Read From The Bottom Up]

Poets, know we never wanted that
Not even a poem can knock us down
but we got what we got; we stand ready
Old guys don't have as much inventory

-

is about what you're not holding now
at the exact same moment, and poetry
we all want two opposite things, always
And I have a secret for you. I believe

-

in such a way that it's newspaper true
I was more than me because you said it
10 or 12 more ghost feet to my height
the invisible things that maybe brought

-

I know have added to my life, safekeeping
All the poets I never heard, never read
their bitter hot tests to wake you up
squishy sweet. And poets are coffee

-

but I love all poets like saltwater taffy
and they got to be hardened steel
Old guys maybe lived on the anvil
a poet is like getting cooked alive

-

becomes a heartburst of love. *Being*
your truck, and lied in divorce court
upside down—the ex-wife who stole
We'll watch it end first, so it flows

-

like a horror when it all departs.
how do poets live? Beauty hurts
of my last consciousness. *Tell me*
will collide in noise over the cliff

-

"You'll be Niagara Falls." Memories
Hope I do *What would a poet say*
volume of gone Hope I don't feel it
My fear is the poetry of that moment

-

then appear for welcome embraces
until you're finally empty. The dead
of flowers that drop one by one away
that feels wonderful. Each an armful

-

it's goodbye to family and friends, love
terribly visible, as you die annoyed, then
You read what's not been crossed off
list wallpapered to the inside of my head

-

There's a lot left to do, and it hangs there
fear of dying, but more running out of time
If I drink too much, it's not that old feverish
and one by one, I stared all but one down

-

I started this world scared of a lot of things
because you can't ever match it in happy
Listen, you can't be sad and sad for long
we stay happy after a good car camping trip

-

I shortened mourning to same number of days
it's all just ticks of the clock that I was born in
Bad times have come, and they'll come again
I can't fall down, or hesitate. Can't get sick

-

But, people need me. CASH NOW. No moods
I have a lot? Well, the sun comes up, and I go
I'm out of jail with no threat of going soon
car that runs, money for food and beer, plus

-

Ah, how can I explain if I've a place to stay
Get compact. When you billow out, you're cut
Streamline it, man, to carve a sense of control
Just love what you have when it all stays put

-

because their length extends right into trouble
We stop believing in arms to reach out and grab
my teeth must be spring-loaded to have any left
Been kicked around by so many people I trusted

Let's Walk The Walls

Do yourself some damage.
I'll howl the beacon out.
Send your criminal self.
Crawl or skulk.
Wear brief disguise.
We'll do everything but fight.
It's time to drink and drown.
Oasis: wrong side of town.
Simplify to growl.
Instinct knows where to find me.
Just slink around.
When you can't hardly breathe no more,
that's my door.
Lick your lips. It'll open.
Slither right in on that snake of a grin.
We'll rocket on some old NASA fuel.
Then eat down to the bone
until we're good and greasy.
Dance in voodoo curse
until a victim somewhere zombifies.
Kiss in alien invasion.
Make love sci-fi.
Or tangle in maneater vines.
Revel in the wealth of a man
and woman unbound in sync.
Peel off clothes until we're raw stems
rising from onion bulbs.
Rewild the floor.
Test the kitchen table.

Plummet into bed,
hit the mattress so hard
we must swim furiously
away from dead.
Forget rules of 2x4's, gypsum and mortar.
Let's walk the walls out 2 or 3 feet.
Puff the roof 8, 9 floors up.
Blow this house apart.
Let the neighbors watch.
You married water, left for dry money,
walk in sparks of static electricity.
But we're free now, apart.
Dishes, oil changes, broken fence gates,
getting lost on the way to a wedding...
that's what your office guy's trained for.
Me? Demolition man.
Let's walk the walls.

Essay: Reverse Rotation Engines

Our problem is Smokey's reverse rotation engine • We had proof in the non-smoking tire • We live as water weaving its way down a hill • Virgin Birth is certainly Kerouac's "unspeakable wisdom of the individual" • There was only one reverse rotation engine in the race • Everything is something else because definition is a small cup • Words are walnut shells • When my days are done, I'll shrug and say, "You die trying." • Poetry is science, except poetry assumes we already know it • In the first turn at the Indy 500, Stan's car broke in half and flew through the air • Most amazing—his steering wheel gone with the front half of the car—he had the presence of mind to dig his fingers into the shoulder harness • Eddie joked that if Stan ever needed to land on him again, he was welcome • All the poetic towering outside our words • If you ever saw one of Sonny's Pro Mod cars launch, you'd understand Smokey's engine a lot better • We live in gross agreement, never comfortable what a transit bus truly is • Transportation? • Captivity? • Community? • Weaponry? • We emphasize that which we've put into words for a sense of control • We talk to anchor ourselves • We beg each other to confirm • No one wants to read what will take their lives forever • Fundamentalists agree out of fear upon the most popular lies from our past • They allow themselves no receptacle for unpredictable future • Smokey died this year of Leukemia • And Stan was thrown through the windshield of his truck in a head-on collision on a desolate road in Australia—killed for not wearing a seatbelt • Poets behave as if walnut shells have value • We are ill because the tiger is no longer in the bush • A reverse engine throws the crank in the opposite direction • Stan was always quick...even as he talked in front of you, he was planning several turns ahead • Write the poem that will stop war • Don't change the finish line just because you can • Smokey's engine threw the crank in the direction of the inside race track wall • What do I owe my children, and what excuse did I accept in not providing it? • The tiger made us smell the air, listen to molecules landing on leaves, and see the world that thrives in shadow • Chris said it was the greatest race he ever saw, and he's over 70, having attended races every weekend he could find one all his life • The large become football players and kick the small • Good spellers become writers and ridicule the big • Everybody lives as another pollutant until will • Smokey had Stan come to Florida to train him on a reverse rotation engine • Poetry has nothing to do with what it's about • Death comes to brand you, finally and forever, as defeated • I'll tell my children I don't think this has to happen • The only thing that exists is that which is done on will alone • It is hard to defeat the fundamentalists because there is rarely solidarity about the future • Those who do not participate in will are ghosts—pay no attention to them • A reverse rotation engine will roll you naturally into the race track corner • But you need a driver who won't turn too soon, per instinct, or he'll crash • If Stan drove the way he'd been trained all his life, he'd put her into the wall • Art must threaten us—tiger in the bush • You want to be alert this second • All poetry is based upon the transit bus before we all agreed it's a transit bus • The Irish Famine was not about food, but politics •

Profound fun is rare because it's water travelling uphill • Stan rode his custom Harley down to Daytona to visit Smokey during Bike Week • My children hold me responsible for the world, and I am—all of it • Smokey explained to Stan the dangers of a reverse rotation engine • Stan couldn't qualify at the Copper World because a goddamned oil pump kept the car overheating • But, he wouldn't accept a substitute car • He'd have to qualify her in a heat race • I think poets ought to write the way Stan entered Turn 1 at Indy • Poets ought to write as if a wrong line sends them into a wall at 200 mph • Poets ought to write as if tigers could read • Put the tiger back in the bush if you want to live • Smokey's reverse rotation engine won the race • Stan started dead last • Coming out of Turn 4, you could see the smoke burning off Page's right rear tire • No smoke off Stan's car, so he had more tire at the end of the race • God bless you, Smoke • God bless you, Stan • A nation without poetry never means what it says • Page got hit in the head by a sprint car • Didn't kill him, but it hurt him pretty bad • God bless you, Page

Teeth Guards At Night

1.
Spend my final years dreaming hard
of a Mekong Delta kind of vacation,
rare and exotic, crawly green, but, no,
I'll live Orlando faux, dead as tourists
who just want to see things they held
so lightly in postcards from moneyed
friends, relatives who got there first.
Maybe I want this Earth to seize me,
shake me into the final knowledge
of what the hell is going on here
as I depart new population figures
for years when I'm glad to leave
right about when the wars for water
go nuclear, and best of luck
finding any farms south of Oregon.
Goodbye Central Valley. It was good
to eat you. So long Ogallala Aquifer,
and welcome desert back to old
Midwest plains towns, gone to dust
and back again, because a lifetime
is all that our memory's good for.
You see an empty ocean in Monterey
and you think it's blue period beautiful,
until someone tells you whales crowded
that bay so much their breath stunk up
the beach just 200 years forever ago.
Yes, I saw extinction; didn't know it.

2.
So, I got nothing left to do but die.
But, I can't help but feel I fail simply
by dying, as if everyone else alive won.
(Or do they cease to exist when I do?)
All I saw and almost saw I thought
would be mine, destined for me
because I'm the kind to die trying
in a backyard spaceshot, but now
I'm scared I spent the fuel on take-off
and risk pulling up lame...shatter
in the void like so much windshield.
You shoulda seen me in Super 8!
Heard me when I was young! Heart
of a gorilla, body of a fence post, face
stolen off a Dublin choirboy, eyes lit wild
with fireflies. "C'mon, peace! C'mon love
and sharing! Strap back in, we're leaving
on my throw of the boosters switch, my
poems, the way I sail, will ride the seven
continents like an airplane shadow proves
flight to people staring at the same ground!"
Yes! Watch a smokeghost army pour out
of the fuselage to shove this brazen rocket
into a pinpoint of light! Loosen up, gravity!
That was then, my wallet filled with talk.
Now, a 55-year-old man waits, ironing
his pants quietly and without complaint,
the wife coiled on the couch, crying raw
slivers of sound from the lupus, human
voice shredded like so much cabbage

for coleslaw, living in alien life form
surely! Yet, still no space ship lands.
Movies unreel in blood red afterimage
on a burning retina. She's Ingres nude,
wanton as a jailbird in an Oakland motel,
rising from the sheets like a flesh island
that Ulysses once glimpsed in fitful sleep
too gone from women to ever lie quiet,
because that's the way she once was.
Made our stand here. Here changed.

3.
And these old hands carry memories
of this jerk's neck who threatened it all,
or so it seemed, or I imagined, long
in drink, at a time I had enough future
left to matter. This guy in Marty's Tavern
one night, Mr. Pettybone, told the reason
for all these roads, and how most men
assume they'll go home each night.
But, Mr. Pettybone didn't like that
not one bit, and he told stories
about the other roads built for me,
and now how I sit there, the center
of this world, with few roads traveled
the last 25 years, because, I guess,
I didn't need them. Pettybone got beet
angry, "All those roads for you! Bars
and nightclubs, unlatched doors
to apartments over pools, lovely
women and cheap alcohol thrown

everywhere!" Customers had to pull
me off of him. Crazy guy, but he knew
men like a drunkard preacher, and
no one wants to consider how close
to awful they nearly could have been.
Life sometimes flickers ghostly light as
just something you maybe made up,
like witches who get it instantly but me
it takes 50 years. Could say a man died
and one man got born when I saw
my front door that night. "Still there,"
murmured in briefest prayer. Ain't seen
Mr. Pettybone since, but I wake each day
and check. Cause it's still a hunter's world
where you got the voice of where food
walks—asleep or awake—and when it's you
about to be eaten some way somehow.

4.
Now, most all is dread, and our indifference
kills a poet each night, the way you can wash
the new car and kill a dolphin species. Nosferatu,
come, night black as a Mexican woman's hair,
while stars take the shape of cradles. Let me lay
my neck open for the wonder again, new creature,
as our regular inoculation of sadness prevents
the old kind of power, or we theorize as the clock
turns to syrup workday afternoons. Then, exhaustion
enters the bloodstream and even you hesitate
to bite! The poison in us will make you feel much
as angels must when they pluck dead baby souls

off drone missile shrapnel, peel a handsome man
from the barrel of his brother's shotgun, slide one
woman's soul up the blade of an angry man's
deer knife. They call it soul shock, when God
Himself doesn't do the killing, but still the angels
must collect. Otherwise, the dead make their way.
They don't stay! Souls rain up and out. Angels relax,
unlike the tug to pull a big man off an electric chair.
You know it's a bad world when angels complain
about all the heavy lifting, a world where each man
gets marred with little tombs for spine, stacked
catacombs for backbone, like a prosecutor who
first pictures his lips upon the rape victim, hands
upon her hips. And men who calculate advantage
brutish as a rain of trash can lids, whose pride
of ownership is skin disease (see it in their face),
men uncomfortable until numb, men made dull
from their muscle and size who fight each other
because what else is there? Ah, give me clothes
that hide me well. Send paychecks to the place
I love. Paint my face the color of a wall. Lifetime
being visible has failed. Eraser time has come.
The days you have to tell me when I'm home,
this rack of skin my hovel. Sunken species.

5.
In the old Pacific, perfect waves sublimated
all this—or was it just that I was young—
exploding against the outline of my body.
Meaning, the tide. Me, the moon. A pier
at Aliso now rises from the parking lot

to the wet sand line, torn off at the shore
7 years back, and I stand there, structure
of mostly memory. Yes, a monthly bill
now to forget. Bank withdrawals to one day
never know. And the grimy pocket calculator
I used to figure out my bills each month
will be on a table when someone claims it,
my fingerprints on the grey casing, then
puts it in a box that's never opened again,
marked in broad black strokes, "Dad."
Crazy how the best nightclubs make you long
for hell and family life is yelling each night
to turn off lights. One recurring dream is left.
I don't know why: bottle rockets pounding
a butterscotch sky. Below, a guy who'll live
it all again drives east on the 55. In awe.
I yell down a cloud cliff, struck like a gong
at the loud cold steel of my best advice,
"Hey, buddy! Wear teeth guards at night!"

Stripe The Beast!

What? Poet come alive!
Please! We know the truth
of this simplest, softest

alchemy: You word
the thing! As if you could
stripe the beast

before it's known!
Before the photograph!
We readers offer pliant

faith, the supple sort
of balsa for one carving
with unyielding dreams

inconstant matter. We
must suspect a poet
put starfish so opposite

night stars, after all. But,
what we want to be most,
we sold, for things brightest

in quick promise, easy now.
Yes, our buying sold us,
an impossible conceit that,

but you, most of all, agree
what can't possibly be real
is the truest thing of poetry.

We are Lake Erie, 1960!
Write a poem; Caribbean
all your readers, please

—turn office desks to coral reefs
—in lightning on stone tablets
—a wizard's throw of tiny bones

across page or screen—
and we promise to believe!
Demand our surrender to you

instead! Re-deify the inside
of our heads! Write a poem
that's a trail of food!

And forget that we came
begging, fingers full only
of your same air.

My Unruly Bar Code Data

Tattoo me with a bar code, man,
so I can scan it, and finally read
my price. Yes, "What does it say?
What does it say?" I'd yell out.
You know that moment of light,
before you're disappointed dark,
the brief second you had value,
mistaken time and again, but
you still hope for sticker shock.
Ah, I go back and forth. Life
would be easier to just fit in,
to have the line at the cashier
go breathless in a soft sucking
noise at what the scanner said.
I mean, it's not good to give up.
To bathe in wilderness again,
get the old identification marks
off me, as they build up and
you can't begin to argue what
you aren't. Whatever people say
with their scared fish eyes, you
just have to accept it because
who's got the time, number one,
people don't care to listen,
number two. Like the furniture
I sold years ago, and it was gone,
but it all moved back in!?! And
I've been looking for evidence
of country inside the TV, but it's like

we're watching their planet's programs
and they must be watching ours!
In fact, I think I'm supposed to be dead
and these years are mostly medical mistake.
I'm living proof that science overshot itself.
The bookstore is lined with liters of soda pop.
Young people are stupid in just the right way.
This is serious. I spent an hour deciding
on two shirts and a pair of pants at K-Mart,
and my sister sees me and says, "Where
did you get those clothes—K-Mart?"
I wish for 8-foot long spider legs, so
I could tap somebody in a meaningful way,
hairy and extraterrestrial, so they would turn
and be glad to see it's just me. This is free,
troubled, but it makes a lot of sense to me.
Don't sit there puzzled. Scan. Price. Pay.

Once You've Been In Love

A woman's hair moves at one-tenth
its former speed, like lace curtains
billowing off a shock of window
on a most uneventful day, the way
you sometimes might see summer rain—
a wave of linens hanging from the sun.
And the older you get, it doesn't part,
just compresses, as you start to dwell
beneath the shed of moments falling
over you—pile of wet autumn leaves.
Someone finally asks, "Can you ever be
in love again?" But you're at an age
when you must confess, the distance
to this life in love is too far for, "Yes."
And then you lose your fear of death.

Jolly Roger Inn

Hell yes, announce my age. Then crash
the cymbals! Look, lightning lines my wallet!
Meet one man who ain't worried about his bills!
Makes me bigger than mere you, every human
occupying the same brief amount of space
so we cannot be judged on square footage!
She's good looking, yes. But cash is prayer
that gets answered over and over. I talk, too,
like a man who drowned doubt in the river.
Knowledge was never in this man's world
about anything except how to get it done.
Here let me pay for this. I learned just how
to say...just when...as she leaned over
to wash the table with her bar towel...
"No tan lines, I like that." Yeh. Keep my money
in my eyes. I'm seeing her tonight. The ex-wife
calls me to say again how I'm old and ugly,
but I run my finger along this life and check
for dust. Still clean. Speck free. All in place.
My age may be ambulance sirens, buildings
imploding all around, but for me, you'll find
sunlight and moonlight work in shifts
to watch one man walk on,
walk straight on.

Us The Poets Us

In language, I proclaim myself,
er, um, differently. Color of eyes:
Mercury. Hair: Dry winter hills
laced with concrete highways.
Favorite song: A Train Whistle
Made My Bedroom Curtains Cry.
Only obstruction to all my lies:
some day, honest, I, too, will die.
Spent this life proclaiming
in language, atmosphere of action;
poetry, final words before space—
a far wider expanse of us,
5 generations later us,
this one planet only us,
us inescapable from us,
us the only lobbyists for peace us,
us begging food, then water,
us who'll put a stop to us,
mothers, fathers, aunts, uncles,
us isolated by love of us,
us unharmed by us,
us who believe in us.
At the outer reaches, atmospheric edge,
there is a poem, how governments renege,
how the ancient feuding tribes—nostalgic
for violence, uncreative from hard distraction—
refuse leadership at the cost of their children,
how all the rich first ripped out their eyes,
how action is small but, some of us breathe

possibility and bold proclamations that, yes,
it can be done! 5 miles above our earth, over
the soil of what we do, cut the poets open.
See how they work. They breathed there first!
"Extravagantly different sort of us," a poet
once proclaimed, where words serve as air.
"Still, we find it hard to breathe, troubled
from the profane ease of simply saying it."

Customer

The cash register rings agreement beyond
friendship or language. A shrug of a woman
has clearly stopped hoping, as she hates
the curl of her hair, its color, and her places
where the body jiggles anarchic as she walks.
I hope for the best for her, but don't talk to me,
lady, because I've got friends and family
who have screwed lives into little hooks,
throwing problems that attach like velcro.
You, yeah, you, stay unknown. And go.
Sure feels like pure desert here, despite
light fixtures and signs and linoleum,
because we don't acknowledge each other
as anything more than ghosts behind
the money, and what we'll trade it for.
Wallets and purses, paper and fingers
asking a machine if the deal's fairly settled.
A newspaper hovers across the counter,
53 cents, with tax, Armageddon type and
photos of twisty faces, jagged glass—
179 KILLED IN BALI BOMB BLAST.
Tell these dead and their families to go, too.
My eyes reeled it in, and my brain played
the slasher film on a back wall of my skull.
I identified errant shades of black as blood,
body pieces, brick and the pit of human loss.
I would say something happened just then,
although, if you were right behind me,
you'd swear nothing did. The math of it.

10,000 miles. Complete lack of flesh.
All the people who don't know what to do,
which, I think, is all of us. Events strike,
and resonate. Transaction completed.
Next in line. Next in line. Next. Next.

How to Grin Down A Bar

The only bar worth grinnin' down is grizz,
but good luck finding one, all dead since 1910,
except for East of Yellowstone. So, first
make airline reservations, but make them fast,
at least four weeks ahead, because they're crazy,
with rates according to the exact minute that you call!
And people in emergencies, with no time, get killed!
Now, if you do just what I said, you'll get eaten,
because you have lard for brains listening to a fool
poet tell you what to do in the wild. Bears smell that.
So, better yet, drive a 1200 cc Classic BMW motorbike,
although my friend argues you should tear it down
and build it up before you leave, to drench
yourself equally in both discipline and abandon
so the bar can't smell you because you're awful.

Maybe I never actually grinned down a bar,
but I'm fearful of what might happen if I don't,
afraid the whole thing will go out. My worst fear
is that desire doesn't come from blood or
nerve lines or somewhere in my goo circuitry.
What if desire is just a guest in the house,
and it decides to go back East, just to see Miami
for a while, or Door County in the Wisconsin thumb,
for the fall, and desire might like it there?
I assume my skin and bones would collapse
like a fireman just leaped out of his suit.
A man writes fraudulent bar grinnin' poems
because every poem fails, but what do you do

with a fear so big, it's weather; bigger fear
than tornado chasers ever saw; bigger than winter;
more like the havoc the dead cold of a meteor might cause
…out there….out there…aimed still at my planet.

Empty Oil Barrels

Calypso? Ex-slaves welded
junk the masters left behind
to outring cathedral bells,
music the heart's corona.

Just like me and fast. Hell,
with two empty oil barrels,
I'd bolt up a Flintstone car,
find all the speed no money

can buy on the dry side
of the continental divide
and coast her to a stop
in the middle of Bonneville.

But, all this jazz and zoom
always has to fight for life
as it blooms from nothing,
and no one wants that. Why?

To me, money's dull as paper.
but my girlfriend, angrydrunk
in her college's cornball pub,
said, "You go right ahead—

be a mechanic! And spend
this life washing your hands
from the grease and blood
of hunting precious power!"

Most folks speak a baffling
language. So, I must guess
what she was trying to say,
"I don't understand 185 mph."

But that's just the way life is,
like the sun is a hole, ablaze
with invitation for you and I
to get our bare skin to glow!

And if we fail, let's fail once,
twice more! You know...
the physical as trampoline,
water as a lesson about dust,

dead of cash across the palm,
utter lack of words for true new
things getting done. Maybe this:
same as priests hunger for a kiss.

Taco Tuesday 11:35 p.m. Promises

Fingertips of softest octopus suction cups
or whirring little wheels of fur. And maybe
just a drop or two or three of deep sin oil.
Nail my tongue to the exposed garage wall
and step back, then step again, until a good
three, four, feet of licking's left. Rhythm
of dogs, dolphins, horses, atomic clocks,
roofer hammers, hurricane shutters
loose on a Class Three, stutterer stuck
in an Independence Day speech on flag,
freedom, fireworks, f, f, f, f. Beg Vishnu anew
to haunt my flesh then write His holy verse
in you, again and again. Better yet, in 20 years,
I won't be the one yelling for goddamn salt
and pepper at my end of the dinner table.

Nature of Time in Las Vegas Airport

Time eddies and whorls in an airport bar,
and he's questioning whether he's here
or not again. In grey, pleated cotton slacks,
pressed cotton shirt, company logo embroidered
red over his heart, he's maybe everything else,
fixture along with bartop, barstools, and light
upon the liquor bottles. Or does he alone
enjoy the basketball game and beer, longing
for a bowl of nuts and wishing the bartender
would just shut up? What's time when you work
the patron's job...hell, any job? Who exists,
when a person paints the table and all decor
as much as the checkered flag floor, neon "Pit Stop"
sign purpling three walls, along with race photos
of Earnhardt and son. A hidden poet, he sits, slurps,
and is the only human here haunted by the ceiling lights
refracted high in the waiting area windows, holy cubes,
boxes of bold errant light, geometries of heaven,
as if you saw a thing in eight dimensions at once,
and lived. Yes, haunted! The sight won't exist long
without a poem, he thinks! Magic is because of us!
Still, this is always a box of strangers. One more hour,
they'll be gone, but the airport bar remains the same.
A man picks up a briefcase, heads to the terminal.

Panic Attack

We go through this life bumped
by balloons that get gone soon
as we turn our heads to witness.
We can lean on another world.

We're shadowed by a dome,
can't be entered, no door, no,
you reach inside your own
chest and rip yourself inside

out by the heart chakra, then
you're in. This house surrounds.
Or, at least, that's my theory,
because no life's well lived

on protection, temp, calorie.
I'm trying to say that I imagine
a fishing boat a half-mile off,
holds my dead brother, same

as heaven, place afloat away.
Jah love put him there for me
to be close as he is happy. And
in Jah love, we pray, make us

green and easy as river moss,
fragrant swamp monster sex,
crowded cloudwalk, cypresses—
early morning Everglades a sign

Jah love forgives. It must be!
Well, my parents despise me—
I won't take Dad's crap. My kid
crashed a car, my work declares

there's a line of people desperate
for my job if I lack the dedication
to spend the hours—I'm at 70 now!
Last night, driving through the canyon,

I think I had a panic attack, not knowing
what it is, but I thought I would breathe
myself away, until an empty car hit
the oncoming traffic, and people

were puzzled how it ever got that far,
just empty space behind this wheel.
Jah love, forgive me. Salmon scales
mid-leap bright sun, silver me.

Benbulben heather, blue me.
Mohave sky, hawkdive me, please,
that I might be forgiven as the trees,
if poetry might count these days

as proof of impeccable behavior,
in place of sacrificing children.
Send a poem opens us home
beyond the contract of senses.

Jimmy The Lock & Dream

Gone Gladys jimmied the lock and dreamed
fast of escapey type things, no recollection,
no crawl of past, just a movie of all want,
filmed with stuff and places and nobody
she knew in it, all available! Even the sun
hung temporary, like she could remove it
to hang over the blue sofa, or in her garage,
or hand it over to a lover, a bum in a box,
her Grandma, whoever, meaningful things,
free if you had heart enough for the cash
laying a couple hard yards from a window,
easy as morning, a new language awaited
as she could talk in money, or in objects,
in things actually in her hand, instead
of a magazine or a blur of money or sex
on TV that she almost saw, always felt.
She could float, and wave to everybody
as who she truly was, in pictographs
sprung loose from grimey skull walls,
in a metallic "SPROING!" "Oh, yes,
I have all this!" she'll say "I once lived
so unadorned, I don't remember why.
It was courage bought all this, and fast
hands, grace. Now I have identity, not
missing limbs, unknowable name,
no credit, toxicity of being discounted."
Yank the cashbox! Or you *must* believe
in reincarnation to pay for this waiting.

Tropicana

Balls of breath ellipsed out lava lamp-like,
a cotton spun of Coors beers, Marlboro Lights
that pressed into the window, then stuck.
"Las Vegas is a lonely star," Mitch slurred.
Get away from the window! Or maybe
I should just shove him out! I swear
everybody over 50 is husband and wife,
in anxious intimacy from getting pounded on
all these years, like I saw you in the hospital
and brought you a bed pan once, and you
had to tell me I was drooling on an airplane.
We know all this, but it gets worse:
there's no point in talking about it!
Einstein didn't invent enough time
for us to help each other at the end!
Mitch has a grainy moon face right now,
hard grey, cratered, darkening beard.
But the failed eyes are too much. I wish
we could put eyes in a jar overnight, or
I could just get ahold of his and put them
in a cabinet. "Why should I give the projections
tomorrow? They're just going to can me!"
Like I care! But, the fucks made us share
a room to save money, and now he's mental.
They don't pay me enough to watch a man cry.
My luck to be there every time someone gives up.
Or are people just giving up all over the place?
Some guys don't die. They melt back to plasma.
"Mitch, I'm turning off the light. Watch TV

for as long as you want. I'm not your Annie."
(Russ, you fat bastard, I'm pissed at you, too.
Where's that Super Bowl bet? I'm putting you
in every poem until you pay up, you jerk.)

Caldera

(1)
In this life, they throw a switch:
one day you're living would be,
the next you're living was.
The manna's in what's done.
Thinking? Inhale. Exhale. Yes,
Jules' history was of breathing.
Ay, carumba! Could he breathe!
While the new world that he wanted
roiled round and round, unchanged.

(2)
Angels always breathe above it all,
let demons build the killing train,
the food no longer running
wild on the western plains,
angels careless to the eating, demons
cooking resurrections on a hot plate,
in a spice that burns down doors.
Angels fly for anyone's approval,
while devils desire so much more
that damn if they don't get it!

(3)
The day they threw the switch,
Jules finally found a poem
is a shove, paper sure caldera.
What had Jules been thinking of?

(4)
We'll send our boys to war
to keep the oil pipelines ours,
an ours 5,000 miles there.
Heat the ocean into sipping tea.
Kill off all this quirky cosmos
with our shrillest forms of fun.
A culture gone cadaverous,
while he theorized and noted,
got pissed off and roared,
his finest thoughts balletomanes
at the Battle of the Bulge.

(5)
No more. His poems would rise
and punch...elbow their way around!
Yes. Death to stop and think.
As if we must first faint.
First learn to lie down
for hours on the roadside.
"Poets! Face it! Events
vaporize all we try to say!"

Let's Rub

In L.A., we found a way to breathe from somewhere
behind our heads. We can smell a new way to dress
one beach back. The air and light hold onto the sun
at night, until it, too, is mostly clothes, haircut, wildass
hope, so you're strutting into the Rainbow Room straight
out of the sun's chest, but it's a sun like you—dark coat,
grey T-shirt, ready to explode down all the alleyways,
a sun that had an uncle supernova'd once, a corner sun,
await in the palms of concrete and streetlight,
targeted, yes prey, yes, in worship of its predator.
So, c'mon! C'mon! Pick Melrose up, and put it on!
Bend Venice down into her freaky love. Fun
Santa Monica in the ferris wheel sun helps
our parents to hate us way more than once,
but we answer, "Young flesh is cash!" Keep
your purchase of our mere politeness, thought
follows short skirts & tight pants for memories
yet to be had of ecstasy and release and freedom.
You know it one night, and your lamp gets lit.
(Let's be cruel to the old, and show more skin.)
Make Sunset your runway, your next lover
the U.S. Senate, every Whiskey band you ever
heard your own Department of Loud Defense.
Can't think straight. Can't love. Let's just rub.

Essay: Choice As Artifact

You believe it is immoral to express Boredom. • Just as in the environment, time can be polluted, too. • The Controlled Moment is denuded landscape. • It is the tree fallen across the trail that makes wilderness experience so exuberant; there will never be a fallen tree in Disneyland. • The world operates in fractals: We repeat our sexuality over and over, in all manner of activity and relationships, until we have something larger—culture—that is essentially the same thing. • Today, there are 'courtship rituals,' with artists seducing and audiences receiving, but there is rarely consummation. • The poetic moment is orgasmic. • In a Shaman Culture, knowledge is orgasmic/ecstatic and not available merely by acts of purchasing, such as tuition or seminar fees. • In a Merchant Culture, you will always align yourself with accumulations of wealth. • Counterculture is co-opted immediately as marketing tool. • Mass media buys only enough creativity to prevent the Bored from rising up and seizing methods of cultural production. • We are hardwired for poetry, just as we are for laughter and music. • Boredom is toxic. • You are most comfortable being presented with a choice between two displays of accumulated wealth. • With advantages in scales of volume, corporations only use the most expensive technology for products of human expression as an empty but powerful way to sell tickets, but it will be calculated, bankrupt of profound ideas and devoid of surprise. • Expensive technology in human expression is the same experience as constructing an office building—paradigm of marketing and finance. •

Mass media must present a sense of order, even when none exists. • In addition to ill health, Boredom is 'horny'—a blessed and natural jones that won't just go away. • Your favorite movie star is an office building lobby, and the summer blockbuster is a chemical dump of Controlled Moments. • What we want from art is the predator back in the brush.

Why Spring Hurts

A canopy, my dream,
of ferns caressing walk,
and a moon practiced

in the whisper of light,
until a stranger comes,
offered by the jungle.

A senseless man laughs,
takes nothing of import
and shares it as bread

with hungry believers
in impossible collusion
with all aimed and open

to the sun. Simple! A dizzy May
mesmers, they agree to anything,
and we eat the poet's reveries.

Let's make a poet Marshall,
then beat out wild new laws
to jail the well-heeled unwary,

sure and certain oafs, and
anybody ever mean to Mom! Yes!
Life to the unlisteners! Oh,

and you should know your smile
arrives so far before you,
the wet grass is already trampled.

Audience

Oh, the gray palazzo, veined
in crepuscular vines, still bossing
the Genoa cliff around, yet

weak as we'll be from history,
when we stole in.
The cold tugging at me, inside

the sleeping bag, through the tile,
a gravity of dying.
You were my muse back then. You

who never ate a pomegranate,
never pitched a car sideways in the dirt,
never read Lorca.

The genesis of gods must begin like this:
both your hands gripping the marble
of the window ledge, so you could add a lover,

enormous moon filling you so, in front, hips
ham-smacking hips behind (what tented tribes
must hear each night), radiating a fibrous glory

of steam, sweat in static heat, huffing
quick, rough clouds into the porcelainic light.
What we must have looked like!

Yesterday, I announced all this
to a coffeehouse, then sat down.
I must have left something out.

How I dropped epiphanies for paychecks,
tired so of doubt, and in all good sense,
no longer take full measure of the sun,

how I am not sad, in the imprecise discipline
of family life, I am not one thing or another,
and despite a wife-and-children's fears,

there's no memory that owns me,
how I can't be derailed by this, how
I neither stay nor run away. Yes,

I recall my wreck of hands, holes in every view,
horizon upon horizon, after your divine taking
on a bartender's smoking Moto Guzzi.

Another time, I announced this, too,
but I think they want me suicidal, unmoved
at a joy flawed by all that happened.

So, next time, "Save me,"
I announced. All I did was live—
spent now of adventure,

my poetry of pleading—
"Save me." Voice, so devoid of lullaby,
augurs silence. They stood. Applauded

Geography of Buttons

Flat, faded moon, color of old teeth,
secured small against the nakedness
we fear so much, a tiny "Stop," or
unlatched fast when we say, "Go,"
to touch our way to freedom. Crazy

how this glint of bone barely there,
describes our one minute yes one
minute no approach to clothes, life,
sewn machine right, threaded tight
as if by little children, exported sins,

a technology so old you can't believe
you wear it still (what awaits life after
buttons?), the Middle Ages purchased
with a Citibank card, bulletproof...
everything else designed to break.

One day, maybe our first fastener
will be plugged into the power grid!
Now, it's a disc of a dead cat's eye,
albino plastic, one of the first feels
for my fingers each morning, daily

dreary tasks before work, complete lack
of enigma, satellites for wrinkled planets,
last bit of apparel without logo, quick
picket fence against trespass, bleached
stones up a heaving creekbed, mute little

guards that disassemble quickly, ivory's
ne'er-do-well cousin, mother of pearl's
plain-faced bastard of a son, diffident
in the face of fashion, puritan simple,
hedonist pills. If the sky softly rained

buttons how we'd love their sound off
the pavement! Hell, you could throw
handfuls of them like rice at a new bride,
or melt them down into new fingernails.
Put buttons in the palm of a dreamer

and you'll wonder why you have ears,
so much sense and nonsense, it's no
wonder we have parasites in Sierra
streams, same as this, no? A poet
is much less bones than mud! You

dream stupid or don't dream at all?!?
Had a sleep that felt like pavement,
but I've got fingers like a bee hive
on a keyboard to take something...
collapse probability to a thing!

Like the woman who channeled
all the prayers from Soledad, and
said, "The way a SoCal winter creek
is shallow after a day of rain, but it
still knocks you off your feet

and drowns you. They find your body
in the ocean because that's where
the creek goes." Or learning French
from a voice on the stereo: you fail
to keep up if you take time to translate.

Just sit there long enough, and know it!
Not like the media world, where it's told
who is clergy, who is sacrifice, who is idol,
and when is worship. All news, after all,
is, "Hurry. Come with us to die." Honest

to tell a single other person I stare down
my jeans the Cliffs of Moher, my shoes
disappeared in ocean fog, and the wild
Atlantic awaits before I can ever see you.
Eventually, old men write of the benefits

of betrayal. If the true vision doesn't come,
every day's schedule envelops in wet leather,
shrinking. The work days feel like bound feet.
Age becomes your reason to be tired, then
you give up. Surprise! Every drowning victim

dead of exhaustion! You loathe the train come
so far for you to board because it took so long.
She told me every day is an embryo to enter
—slime, muck and mire. It's where you live
to see the world, and if you're at all good,

you still have time to grab the ill-formed,
stickly leg and refashion it to wing. Yes,
the burden is to believe, but look at all
that comes alive in a handful of buttons
when we blow things back to probability.

Essay: Synaptic Media

Because of technology costs, Mass Media is pre-approved by a single individual of accumulated wealth—king or corporate CEO • Legend is free, requiring only the approval of each individual who retells the story • History —product of Mass Media—and Legend tell different truths, different lies • In Merchant Culture, Synaptic Media is mistrusted because the message is not delivered in a display of accumulated wealth • The Internet is the Planet Earth getting wired with a central nervous system • Earth (Gaia) meets the scientific definition of a single living organism, and now is evolving a brain— consciousness • An idea exists in electronic mail and travels only as far as each person operating their PC chooses to pass it along • While Mass Media is a shotgun model, in Synaptic Media, the message is a single 'bullet' that carries enormous power • The message 'leaps across,' or shoots through, an individual to another individual down the line • By its nature, poetry is complex, profound and bold—never a product for Mass Media • Because of the expense involved, Mass Media Marketers are motivated strictly by fear of looking stupid • They only invest in the most minute variations possible of what has proven profitable • CYA • In Synaptic Media, the idea, the meme, will reproduce in the minds most fertile for it— individually, one at a time • There are people horny for the profound, the complex, the bold • Synaptic Media is the winds of weather, the ocean currents, that carry new meme life • This life engine has been wrecked in Merchant Culture because Synaptic Media is a poor conduit of marketing messages (the dumb, the boring, the untrue) • Whatever happens to Planet Earth environmentally happened first in culture • The grim parking structure is built by the grim • In Shaman Culture, Synaptic Media thrives because we value what makes our brains most buzz and pop • These particular memes likely reached you through people with whom you share joy • Mass Media requires technology and calculation to be profitable • Synaptic Media requires faith and magic • Poetry on the internet is right brain activity of Planet Earth • If you sense the heat and weight of synaptic fire, aim the voltage at a like-minded individual

What

What I like about you, honey, is your curvy, mezzaluna grace way of telling lies like there was a turpentine for everything you paint and a world washes this way and that, it runs, as you change your mind to argue you never did or you never were, all witnesses just sonic furor against the truth of right this minute, three gin & tonics into Thursday night with a hopeless but happy man who believes you. The trick of pinball, the winner that stands there the longest just banging the table, wringing all the bells and lights out of the system, the havoc over in the corner that was so quiet all day, all week, until you get in there and lose while hammering out a creation kind of racket so points don't truly matter. There's a line of men and women angry at you, bean counters in this life who have never seen a smile like that, and they skip over it, because value is a committee thing, and there's all the big noise about homewrecking and betrayal, while your smile rolls out a dimension that's gone so fast, it sucked things away with it, then a new smile unfolds from somewhere else, some other universe, the way physicists dream their muses then forget. I'm woozy, and I know I can't escape it. But I come from way over there, so I'm riding your next big bang grin home to all my old convictions. One more cocktail, though, and the elation factory closes down. You're gone to tell a cowboy what his Wranglers do to eyeballs, your company collapsed to crushed cigarettes rimmed red as a bankside curb, while I can't figure another way to travel through space and faith and time. Ha! Weary, drunk nation...as if wormholes emit mysterious rays of language.

My Greatest Poems

I will this life
to a blankness
wild and alive
as albino tiger skin.
And so poetry is
but poor practice:
Words hunt
and fornicate
on the stillest
winter ground.

Light alone etched proof
I ever was: Cash in
the house and leave little
but photos of me—things
I didn't even do!
No time to learn poetry
shines neither bold nor
rich as leather strung
in grizzly teeth.

As if, with no knowledge
of automobiles, we stand
outside a hardware store
window, staring
at the tool display
when a '59 Caddy sails
across the glass.

Thus, my greatest poems
in order, have been:

"Chrome Trim"

"Taillight"

"Fin"

The Purple Martini Glass Is A Brave Idea

M. rode the bullet train, Paris to Dijon—countryside smeared harder every year.

Cows turn to jetting birds. "How speed switches out recognition!" marveled M.

Animals that made us stop and stare, and hope and worry, long gone;

what we worshipped killed off back when we were only walking, running.

"This thing obliterates entire valleys," thought M.,

before returning to his magazine article on stemware.

Only an inconsequential voice, sound of the extinct, would say it:

Mon Dieu! He speeds straight to reading product advertisements,

poems long gone from the grey veldt in a commuter's hands!

Afloat On A Window

He first learned to apply poetry when he took the window out to sea. It'll be a jinx, they said, but what fear has one who's free. And when the waves rolled in, he had to taste. The gulls that harbingered land terrified him each night, in dreams, and the first one he was able to catch, he ripped apart with his teeth. It tasted like a long work day. Uniform, old coffee and one distraction after another. Take a train they said, but you know him. Window, tides and wind. What is strength in a straight line? What is destination? It's all about the specific caress of a day. Remember when he named the band, "Lost Dog Reward," because the signs were already posted all over the country? It's like that. In the politics of nature, the voting's done. The letters and words blow over us in wind tunnel test. They crawl us as if we were posted to our ears in ant hills. Stop for a while, and proclaim as prophet's truth what has no meaning for you yet. Know it first. The cargo of the cruise ships is lost. In the hold of this window, is the chance of being here, he thought. As they watch from the deck, they only fear the sea's vastness if he's in it. They're more food for the horizon, while he lets every day mark him, charcoal to a prison calendar, content to be so written on.

Muriel thought she could lose 85 pounds or marry the Marine. An unknown flu causes her weight, but his death photos freaked her out. It was not a night for deciding, though. Regis Philbin's antic voice ran from the TV room wildly around the house. He had the huckster rhythm, that's for sure, but it's soothing, the sound of home, American prayer. The weather was quiet as a schoolgirl. No urge. Another night when you didn't need eyes or ears. That sort of cruise ship. Without portholes. That sea. Without wave. She sheathed her arms into the pink, chenille robe, sashed it up and walked down the amber hall, ready to tell her Dad to go to hell again if he so much as whimpered. Lorca comes later, his hand pulling her to sleep.

"With darkness around her waist, she dreams on her balcony, green flesh, green hair, with eyes of cold silver. Green, how I love you green, under the gypsy moon..." Lorca allowed himself to know the thing first. Talking about why she's green puts you on the cruise ship. There's some weird, weird, unspeakably weird 'how' to Lorca. So big, it can be the basis for an entire culture, as pervasive and all-encompassing as the one we're in. And if we merely tell the poet, "I like your work," or we read it in the middle of the night and don't say anything, we're still on the cruise ship. We haven't 'read' the poet, despite our desire.

He flagged a freighter to Galveston. Greyhound bus to San Antone. Build sacred objects for exiles. What else is poetry for? If only to unzip the skin down your spine and finger the thing that makes you feel out of place, everywhere: This is not my language; not my dress; not what I was raised to do. He knew this God, this Everything. Opens its eyes, perhaps asleep still. It probably didn't even see him. And the eyes close. And that's it for his life, because no one has the geo time, eco time, for the eyes to open again. But, he knew one thing: We are living in an era where exiles may hold the same, sacred object, and be vastly alone, with hundreds of miles between them. It's the opposite of two long lines of refugees greying down a dirt road to the horizon. It's why they don't have a big Museum of Protest somewhere, although he'd travel 3000 miles to see it. Can't surrender, can't ever win. Travel in mystery. Only to find his country when he names it. It's the shadow of the sacred object of exiles that serves as compass. Hold the thing in the sun. Search for the ground within it's shadow. There's our country.

At night, he practices sleeping in the bosomy hand of God.

Tatiana wore diaphanous fabric the color of twilight. Merely. Which is the physical nature of poetry. Brutely. As she walked toward the bed, light from a wall lamp rose on her face. Hands, arms, face lit warm as August wheat fields. Her body remained in dusk. Only. As if it is between day and night, only, brutely, merely, we can see in her sky Saturn, Jupiter, Venus, planets round and easily forthcoming as they are, with no need for the anxious sparkling of starlight. What would make him halt and wonder again with all his being? Oh, Tatiana. And there's a wonder in everyone like this? Like a Sears store—wide open and busy with customer—housed in the dark of an underground missile silo. She sunk into his arms, and it wasn't lyric.

This happened to him once in Laughlin, Nevada. Poetry makes you feel close to another real as the third red 7 in a slot machine stopped just above the payoff line. Perhaps this other real we sometimes sense in poetry is another culture, another way of living. The 7 hangs there long as a busted guillotine blade. And there it stays. No amount of want would deliver its announcement of real fortune. No rackety greed bongo solo in the slot machine well. We can ponder the promise of that hanging 7, but it's still a planet suddenly and forever at mid-spin. The feeling of being that close to wealth. Lightheaded. Nearly swooning. But, what begins as wild desire or chance, evolves into objective. Same thing with poetry. Readers insert their silver dollars, pull the handle, and stay there until three in the morning because, occasionally, they sense a physical closeness to objective. An objective that has to do with what? Another culture entirely? He thought that was so sexy it made him want to fuck. The waitress' flattened calls of "Cocktails...Cocktails..." could have been his name. A poet in Laughlin delivers two sevens to a jackpot, amen we pray.

He never saw so many emotionless faces as in the circus glow of slot machines. But, the casino will never deliver all those jackpots, and neither will poetry. The reader is not easily acquitted of a poem. To allow the reader to sit by the slot machine is to fail miserably in what poetry is about. Poetry is about movement. Poetry is about sudden disembarkment. Poetry is about embracing. And it is totally one-sided: Poet is owed everything. The price of a book of poetry is always nothing. Instead, the debt the reader must pay is always physical, or the reader remains barely human. The reader must feed the poet, house the poet, fuck the poet, dance with the poet, hand the poet another Bud, kiss the poet warmly on the cheek, or there never was a poem. Poets can't allow people to be readers —dancers reduced to grazers alongside the abattoir.

Rain drops splattered green and crystal off the mulberry leaves outside. He had been alone for seven days thinking of what to write. Furniture, by now, had grown twice its size, leaving little space to walk between rooms. Doors had grown smaller, rounder. Walls murmured yellow crowd noises to each other. Most contented moment: sliding his thumbnail down a wet Budweiser label, in a Seattle bar by the fish market, until it was fabric clearly torn for anger and sex. A fisherman's wife watched over her husband's shoulder as he drank, and the three had this ideal, immobile relationship for 10 or 15 minutes. Everything functions as it must when too far to touch. The guy paid the bill and the couple left. She looked back at him at the door; poetry is not the moment the body washes up on shore. This joy in finding, grief in parting, all the damn doors. Maybe he couldn't write well enough to make her appear on the porch, what if he could? Her squirrelly thing is men fearless of the ocean. But, first, to announce his sea. It was Western Avenue. Full length of it. But how? Whoever had the smell of Ida Mae's sweet potato pie boiling sweetly in the brain pan, eternal as Loaves & Fishes, that's who, that's where, that's how.

"Lovers, stay!" When you arrive in the center of the ring,

embrace, strip, fall to canvas, and things are licked, rubbed, sucked and entered, he doesn't know what to call it. Yeats let it have one line, "How can we separate the dancers from the dance?" Why April is the cruelest month. That is his heartbreak, this referee's voice, calling for so much to remain still, to just freeze in the corners until the bell. His arms outstretched, back bent slightly, head turning left and right to check this moment of apart. The hesitation can be explained, while the consummation relegates words to cupboards below kitchen sinks with detergents and cleansers, old sponges, potato cleaners, dish strainers. More than fraud—having no words for it. This life of yelling to stay still. This derelict constancy. What manner of monk—or cop—is this, and in whose employ? It is the easy poetry of war. In the end, immoral. But, poetry made him feel so close. To objective. Apple. "Don't mind me." Words were free, and they came fast and violent, street gangs in civil war. His death, now the same as any other. "Go ahead; crash. Form identity fronts on the weather satellites, then tornado. In minutes, in an hour, it is done." Poets will grow criminal again.

Lorca gave her horse's hooves. Gave her father legs, a tourist's smile, easy manner of Spanish plains. Lorca wrote dirigibles. Flight with silky Eurotrash, diseased bohemians, genderless demi-monde one poem away. Lorca wrote sea water, not making her thin but buoyant, amid a cafe full of men who talked more and more of love in ample handfuls with each pull of their rioja. The ones who know up and down their chakras that dance is censored by hipless women. Until her only thoughts held snapping castanets.

Lorca writes a Wild Animal Park for dreams. Lorca writes parrots into sleep sky. Lorca wrote Muriel no longer required dreaming of her father fallen to the floor, writhing in reptilian violence to get back up on his television chair. If only Lorca poems attached to the body —eels of night—to accompany her in daylight. Next day, Tuesday, she left the house for the poetry reading with her father shouting for new batteries for his clicker.

Macheechanga! And what the fuck! The revel broke to raven flight, a caw-caw-cawing from the bones, language but a dam holding surrender back. Our sole commerce was always thus, consume/consumed as one, the way it was milliseconds after the Big Bang, awareness, before it cooled. In words, you ride the brakes. Tatiana could forgive him for refusing the work of merchants and clerks, as long as he mesmerized her with the things here and not here, and stole her off politest avenues to salsa bars where bodies transcend merrily to hellfire. American men never allow their bodies knowledge, yet before her was poet and beast, with the mojitos beating a conga rhythm to driving snakes into the sea. Tonight, giving and taking would be the same thing. Some day, she'll have to kick him out, as he too fails to be immortal. Tonight, spend it all, buy it all. Everything else is nuisance, clutter, detritus dipped in adhesive. Next day, Tuesday, she left for the poetry reading with nothing left to give except her most expensive tears. Afraid. Merely. Mostly.

Wait for churches, wait for beds. Impotent, angry over wordlessness, his only option, history. Better yet, first words of legend. Under the table, up her dress, tugging until she lifts her hips, and he strips them off. Words for this until it's real. Dear reader. Shoves the table. Arm across her hips, pulls and twists until she's straddled in. Poetry...what words alone live like this? Her fingers stacked along both sides of his neck, mouths pressed as plumbing. Tremor. Slightest slide. Undulate. Slicker. Raise her up, unbutton his jeans. Her eyes high upon the wall as she lowers, crushes down. Her shoe heels pointed back at the crowd like new black guns. Whatever happens. Aware opaque. Unzips her dress. She pulls her arms from the straps, dress collapses to her lap. Music stops. Band leader yells. Word, "Couple." Just like she was rolling bread. Her hands grip the red naugahyde until its pink. She releases in blacksmith bellows against his cheek. He releases in fingers tight around her waist. Applause. She moves, pulls on the straps, quickly gets a mojito straw between her lips. He does her dress. Lifts a mojito to the happy crowd. Horns strike out. They turn and dance. Next day, Tuesday, he'll go to his poetry reading, German torpedo to a British frigate, you bet.

Next day, Tuesday, hold of a window, dark corner of the sea, he would read his poem aloud. Across an expanse of gunmetal waves, cruise ship portholes and deck rails painted with expectant faces, the castaway to save these luxe liner hosts. Except he set himself adrift to more poignantly, more prayerfully, more archangel-like, write of rescue. Why else is there to write? As if pleading most artfully would somehow transcend into something else. Only when he wrote did the ocean current course. Other readers said it baldly—"What about me? Witness me. Believe me for once."—pathetic notes from kidnapped kids to alcoholic parents. One person's efforts ended, "Well, fuck you, asshole. You can go to hell." This frontal lack of discipline, determination, insight, care, guts, was surely the aggressive desert in voice. And more. Fault lines cracked the San Antonio bar, everybody grows separate. No one capable of quake. The reason he'd leave Tatiana would be visible tonight. She loved the trying, the getting close, and will despise him for his failure. Waits on a barstool in the back, her legs live eels dangling in bait. Everybody waits. No poem more powerful than the crevasses we make. No poem to weld a bar floor shut. With failure the most we can aspire to, here goes. A purple light shoved him to the mic.

Could I pleased be saved? Western Avenue flowed like a time chart for upper and lower Egypt, except for pool halls instead of Pyramids and a giant donut where the Sphinx might hang his head. The desert sure took it back again. There sure came the Valley of the Dead. Could my pleading transcend to something else? Waves and waves of Israelites. Once, man, it was green. Crocodile walk. Flamingo strut. Cormorants always aiming what they're getting at. Maybe it was the way Immigration stole apartment complexes. Maybe it had something to do with the bust that night at Green's. Who makes the drugs that turn everything to salt or sand. Maybe God just wants an all-night bowling alley, and He left when it shut down. Anthony killed by the cops for pointing with a cell phone. One bullet shoots through neighborhoods. Ida Mae closed her doors to grieve the days away back home in New Orleans, a liquor store in her place. The smell of sweet potato pie gone from the pavement, from the shadows, the corroded air, the cacophony of noises volleyed out from somewhere. His first real girlfriend, Mercedes, gained brief fame as a murdered motel maid. Rafe caught a dime in Soledad. Munch got withered alive. He didn't know how the darkness came, or how it took his friends away. Until the only artifact left of was, was love. His love. Big and bulky, useless as a sack of newspapers around a crippled paperboy's neck. Tatiana sobbing at the back. A woman in yellow, at the side, shifted her 200 pounds to dream. Then, he cradled Western's news. Hieroglyphics of the tomb. Civilization lost, archaeology of wounds. We don't make amends with memory. We abandon it at a bus stop. Doors open without trust. Hell, he didn't get it right. Done.

Yes, there was applause, as for each before him. Eyes did not pursue. He walked out of the collective gaze, which remained fixed upon the mic. He couldn't tell if this was an audience, or animated attachments. If it was up to him to make the difference, he had failed. Tatiana was wiping her eyes with her fingers. At least she allowed the poem to turn physical. Proof of something. And the poem would sure be there in bed when they fucked tonight—heaving sexual device. Yes, she would glory in his company for a while, but the night grows cold so fast. The woman in yellow, standing by a bar rail, took two steps back as he passed, although there was plenty of room. As if he was 10 times his actual size. When he reached Tatiana, she took one hand into hers. It reminded him of a nun a long time ago, before she begged him to stay in school. "You're amazing," said Tatiana. "There's only one of you." The next poet up began, "My telephone did not ring last night. But, you said you would call..." A planet turns to desert in that voice.

Tatiana had sworn off such temporary men, and so it was briefness that made her weep. She could spend a good part of her life listening to him read that poem again for the first time. Briefly, he was perfect. Briefly was his stay. She wasn't going to be like her sister or her brother. Tatiana had the brains, the fortitude, the ambition. Build a life. Construct cathedral from your years. But, love is surely lava in the rock. Every living planet has its molten core. Her and him were destined for caldera. Just like the poem sort of said. Briefly, they were mountain range. Tonight, we'll get so seismic, lava flows. Brief is the night carried with you all your life.

He wasn't Lorca, but he had the body tension of a fireman who's decided to knock down the door of a burning building. God, to even try to be Lorca. The brashness. He did hit some notes, in the realm of reflexes from music or laughter, a trueness that plucks at the strings and guts of who we might be. All the others offered no investment of themselves, as if poetry would somehow be available to them as easily and quickly as a new pair of shoes. He might give his whole life. Muriel would fall asleep with him tonight, instead of Lorca, but only for one night. The poetry reading ended. The poet stepped to the bar. What seized Muriel—a Spanish ghost? Her shyness, her reserve, her fear presented themselves as hothouse flowers, as she watched the jungle get a beer—gloriously green. And his girlfriend? Leave that up to him. A poet deserves all choice. Muriel moved. Whispered in his ear, "I want to blow you in the men's room." His head held a hotel room keyhole and the voice of the featureless girl moved as smoke from a hallway fire. Tat heard it, and smiled a rail station welcome to all. A willing mouth, and the respect of bended knees...the big girl isn't just cruising in coma. Maybe we all just have to share for peace, all the old rules constructed for the quiet of rubber rooms. He kissed the bold fan quick on the cheek; Tat long on the lips. Left it at that. Lapped by waves. Weathered fine by these elements. Knowing still he's only free from the current dead alone. And there's no animated maps on anybody's face to get there.

Leafspeak

Asphalt or concrete entire beneath my feet,
while trees just line the roads alone, divided
as convicts too dangerous to congregate
or grumble in anger over brash new weather.
Neither soil nor sand, forest nor jungle, soften
my footstep or view, while all the food I eat
travels an impossible 1500 miles by tanker
and tractor trailer to my dinner plate, the last
farm of strawberries visible on my way to work
condemned to new cement for condo tracts.
Earth fevers to kill the all-devouring virus
with no other host organism we can leap to
after a blue planet turns lifeless slate carcass.
Where we lived rose up in hurricanes, typhoons,
drought, fire, floods, tornadoes, all manner
of crop failure, disease and dirty water,
oceans, lakes and rivers gone to desert
with far less movement than you'd find
on the broiling sand mid-day, 125° F.
Climate once was a mountain, untethered
now so the Mojave feels free to move over
the Sierra Nevadas into the Central Valley,
great green source of half our food. Worse,
much worse, is now ordained, but unknown
to us who refused to worship undemanded,
and must pay for our easy hubris, as God
will one day make me the trembling leaf
with one glance from Her empty nests.

Bloom The Flower Now

Weather got so electronic, young men squealed,
reprogrammed their ejaculate, DNA rebels
against the analog, in mad hunt for women
who ovulate the hottest new sequencing,
information a god fleshed inside our church.
"Bloom the flower now — control alt delete,"
sung Greta, uncommon in her colors,
appareled in riot, assuming even the toxic
must hold a beauty for those without choice,
"Let me grind my youth upon your lap!"
She lived in a flat above the ladder store,
me raised on aspiration, how were we to talk?
Add 30 years! We need moonshots to meet!
Yet, ugly as I am, there's still a wonder
as she bends to adjust one heel—her hair falls.
Greta had been to college, and she yap-yap-
yapped all she heard there, my protestations
of poet extinction unheard. I knew the drill,
money for years—my boat, my wine, Sony gift,
promises expensed through the ladder store.
Ah, the girl could lay down and fuck, digging
gorgeous new valleys with the roll of her back,
headboard in rigor mortis yet bouncing about,
her lips and mouth believed a lot, a clock
that constantly chimed, "Quarter to climax!"
Would she melt into her history, as everybody
else, until fate gained permission for cruelty,
and set straight to work on her? Life of sinking?
She didn't fall in love with me, nor pretend,

and so, I gave her noise. And hoped it didn't fit.
We were info—too much data flooding the city
to believe in love. Just add it up. Barter myths?
Yes! We'd slide against each other in a way
that delivered. She reveled in being on sale.
I still existed. Judgment obsolete in a pop-up
world. Click. Find us. She's the one
with no tan lines. I make her laugh.

My Friend Hates Poetry

Dandelion fur bounces slow as music notes
to a waltz, as air composes, its fingers on
little parachutes, and I think of a warning
about words in the hands of an old poet.
"They are tools, real enough to give blisters,
or should be!" said a friend, blunt as fish.
Well, yes and no. I am given to daydream,
having turned my brain to cloud years ago,
as if hope is vapor, fun lasts, and so secret
is the love of women for poets, their eyes
are only allowed to message out in blinks—
they stare, blink, and look away—fearing
the loss of control that keeps us fettered
to a life that is mostly calculated to FEED.
Poets chase the cape held before the bull.
"No!" Says my friend. "You take us away,
pharmaceutical-like, so we leave this life."
"Do you love this life?" I ask. "Yes! Eat
a peach, fall down an ocean wave, kiss
before your brain gives you the go-ahead,"
said my friend. "Life! Who needs to give
our appendages to the air? Keep them
on a lover's hands or in a mother's care
of a child's forehead cooking up a fever."
"But, I, uh, er, you know, saw the flight…"
Maybe I am just desperate to pretend.
And I know why. Never told my friend.
Actually never said I, myself, might be
invented. My friend, though, chose

to be my friend. Who is he talking to?
Maybe friendship should give blisters!
"And my cloud is real as your couch!"
My friend, proof of the permeable wall
craved by old poets, sighed, stubborn
as a broken down Coke machine, spilling
and pouring everywhere but in a cup.

Ode To Lovers In Separate MFA Programs

How sweet corroded light had been,
as Hadley summer chrome turned
the color of abandoned pickup tin,
skin nut-toned in Love Lake sun,
glows paler with each day's less.
Our night within the bandstand's ken,
waltzing to the old ones wheezing
plaint, dented trombones gold again,
that final night before school,
when Harvard's lyric wail...
ah, your whip-poor-will ambition
to some day sing a lilting
declaration, "This tree is safe."
The blanket pulled against the cold,
our heat alone commencing us, and now
my turn of phrase, in this—my kiss.
We must not touch until we publish,
love, and I script the dark of Brown.

Blow The Grey Mist

Maybe it was Diz blew euphonious
one night rat brains ESP'd up bar stools
so drunks dreamed of devouring all
after buying enough nerve and zest,
I forget, but I felt it once, a slamming
solo that welded sound with weight,
stole my flesh until I got solely soul.
You can comb your hair a lot of ways,
and get your jacket collar just right,
but don't kid yourself, pal, shakedown
music elevates and plummets your ass,
until you're maybe a single vibration,
and I was scared, all shakey scared,
how a water rises from my lack of faith
like I'm the rain, I'm the river! No one
understands the universe first rang
as a note of music! Doubt destroys
so many dams. My cowardice is
tsunami to the people I love most.
And when the nightclubs and bars
become places I got sentenced,
I chase the outdoors a while, clean up,
see the Grand Tetons tear the bottom out
of a Wyoming sky color of crazy superstition,
skin of a storm sure to flood the Snake,
because we don't know what kills us,
what saves our lives, and we see anger
and punishment, and doubt redemption,
so those greys and whites in the teeth

of a mountain range haunt me chill
as ghost talk...family members dead
and unrecorded tell us to go and hide,
fear that rain until it stops, then join
the shout of blue sky over earth fangs,
delirious one day more, maybe that's all
we get. 10,000 years of art: We have
grocery stores within minutes, food
to kill us, churches run by liars and
pedophiles. Art? We simply refine
the crashing. Bright aisles, blowhard
bellies, cashier priests. No matter.
Let someone blow a grey mist so we
turn finally more than witness—a new
climate to green the hardpack ground.
Resound when this coursing fog comes
your way, tickles you wet one spring!

Excerpt I Memorized From The Rabbit Eye Stories

"Momma, a man's at the door with the biggest, blackest eyes."
Seal eyes! Dear God! Everybody knew that seal in Ponchartrain
grew from an abandoned baby. Now, the unbreakable was here!
It wasn't until Gordon Chiles fell from the sky as a sergeant
that people even knew the seal was gone. What kind of life
is the thing going to lead, landing in a hog farm swamp
from 10,000 feet without a chute, living to tell this tale,
through broken heelbones, ankles, tailbone, shoulder, hand.
It ain't right a man damaged so good remains so alive.
Abandoned baby shapeshifts to seal, then, unbreakable...
Ravenna counted all her kids. What does the thing want?
Many women from the Easy up to Baton Rouge called it
in secret, "Please father my next child. I'll give her love;
you make her unbreakable!" Sort of a prayer, but a man
heard it, holding a black phone to his ear, to answer,
"I'll do it, honey. Be here at 4. Bring your best cassoulet,
and two bottles of apricot brandy." Just like sacrament.
Just like that. Then, gone. Even Interpol couldn't find him.
Now, he's here, thought Ravenna. For my babies? For me?
For everness? "Ravenna, open the door! It's me, Gordon.
I got news. One of the unbreakablettes got run over, killed
dead Charlotte way. No one's safe. No one. Open the door."

Um, Deedee Just Rose Into The Air!

Deedee lit a cigarette, rippled her lips in full
snake hustle with just a hint of millipede crawl,
rang out her disgust, "These eggs are hepatitis!

That ain't yellow, that's disease! Why the hell..."
And with that, she lifted hard into grimy cafe air,
big knees banging red formica loud as careless

furniture movers who air drop heavy cabinets
the final 3 inches, bruising kneecaps instantly
from the way the table was bolted to the floor

to keep regular drunks steady at 2 a.m. exits,
her smoke hung on her lip as if afraid of heights,
then jumped. Yes, she straightened right out,

a puppy held by its neck, her face a signature
of nuclear shock, twisty carnival front facade
to the tunnel of crazy fear, dripping paralysis

of the impossible come anew, how it can't be
for life as we've secured it, life bound tight
as a calf for branding. Remember our lack

of language to describe some moments? Er,
Deedee does, pinned to nothing but the air!
Who knows what it was—our unforetold—

unlike scientists on TV who tell us calmly
when we're all going to die and why, which
we ignore because it's all sensible to death.

Damned? Tell us something we don't know.
Maybe it was a conflux of anger and planets
and the timewave counting down to zero,

as many said it was. Maybe she's a witch
who failed to ever reconcile DNA secrets
with a Central Valley cotton farm upbringing.

Maybe Deedee's aura went all anti-gravity
on her over the sorry condition of her eggs.
Maybe such flight has always been possible

and all we lacked was jet engines of faith.
It was an inexplicable thing for diner eyes tired
already from all their sole memories of pavement

walked each day like a road built by ancestors,
and the grinding strife that serves as the view—
little money and no love plastered everywhere,

construction sites, telephone poles and bus stops...
until Deedee cracked her head on that ceiling!
It announced just how asleep everyone's been!

The crowd stayed screwed down still, a trick
of modern times, to act as if nothing happened.
You could just as easily announce 10,000 dead

in a Hutu uprising, or 20,000 dead through spring
in another sub-Saharan famine, or kids killed
each week in Iraq, and you'd get this reaction:

Look down, look away, it's God stuff, ordained,
a done deal long before any of us were born.
The turmoil and terror we deserve. We ask

for it, or at least, we ask for nothing else. And
one more thing, the eggs weren't all that bad.
It's just that people blow up for some reason.

Pull Out Your Pancreas To Speak

Chip stones into arrowheads or Teton peaks,
as this thing to be said—NOW—hard, sharp,
loud and right as a granite mountain range!
Versus my mush of sentiment, impotence
I embrace as a way to dodge any blame,
all of us imprisoned into talking but one
to another, orderly words line single-file,
a buzzing hive in your mouth but one
bee at a time flies out. I need to shoot
a bullet that zooms 1,000 people but one
victim at a time, because the big guns
have been paid off, the real money in
wasting a world like it's the last junkie.
My memories form a weather system,
while my debt gives voice to every bill
screeching like a flock of blind birds.
I know dead poets crowd the clouds
to shout down a horn pointed at Earth,
but few notice the sound. Junk mass
media voices retell the same old myths,
to set electronic fires in cold nights of doubt,
much treasured inertia hoarded in our caves
as old men choose to melt slowly into graves.
ALL PEOPLE NOT PETS OR FOOD SOON
TO BE EXTINCT. Oh, man, we all must now
announce with internal organs leaping out!
Shout all of our electrons from their orbits!
National Geographic magazine arrives blunt
as a baseball bat: a Dust Bowl mid-century!

We squared the Earth into empty cupboards.
We pulled its drawers and shook them out.
Learn to drink the sand from old creekbeds,
then spit out the taste and grit of the new
climate—wear the feel of thirst like apparel.
Money amputates the veldt from our DNA.
As we cover and hide from the latest news
proclaimed by these raw skies: You're born
for this: Caretaker Species. WHAT? US?

Dig It, Drill It, Cut It, Burn It...& A Poem

No need for potato chips, or comfort of any kind,
after this jelly-fill sort of daydream. Wait. Don't go
all gimlet-eyed. Remember your life led to keep all
debts paid! Yet this day arrives. Not much to do.
Everybody's busy harming someone else but you.
A flowered meadow wet with dew lays full across
your brainpan, some part of you dances through.

And one naturally thinks, who?

Age proves secretarial. You're a thick file to be searched,
but the information grows obsolete. Hope is mimeograph
paper, lightweight, faded, pink, wrinkled. Wad it up. Toss.
You can't play in the NBA. There'll be no Pulitzer Prize.
Name never linked to actresses who deny accusations.

So, leave your wonder where it lies: this turkey sandwich
sure is good. Parked at the marina for free in a '93 Toyota,
watching boats roll past the jetty big and slow as drifting herds.

A dreamer gets shredded up fast as any natural resource
(countries export the life out of their people), until the files
fly off and a drawer hangs open and empty
as a shelf at the morgue. What does a poet do?

With the warmth that lightning gives us,
in the prayer of all sunshine, our hearts
beat out some telegraph shots: end it
now, the way car crashes pardon

traveling salesmen, to give us peace
here, not down that endless road.
We hunt our chrysalis first with a fear
that we might find it, then bank all
our losses, as if heaven held a flash
that could be loaned to us. Finally,
we too fail. (It pleases our parents.
As soon as man could talk, he said
every family runs out of luck. Proof?
Ol' Euripides!) We drape up the real
with all our hopes, but it's, well,
simply a thing that eats. Jesus!
Spears to guns, we got nothing
to send this ravenousness away
in the hell that we dreamed up
because, you know, we want
the beast to be on our side...
fetch us meat...And so, no,
we won't ever let him go.
Hell is where we want to live.
Life is simple for the killers,
no choice outside of murder.
Voracious is our only hymn,
violence holy. Every church
is someone else's abattoir.

Talking Contagion Blues

Minotaurs suggest the flesh is battle ground,
fantasy the wheel that spins our little stars.
Mathematics and all that is but funeral garb.
Firefighters strip suddenly before the blaze,
and exotic female dancers man their hoses,
while TV sausage grinds our dreams to ennui.
Shopping cart or space shuttle, book or menu,
bank account or prison numbers in tattoo,
moonlight jets down upon us its delirium,
then we are what we are beyond cubicles
and the airy promises of quick promotion,
possible wealth, potential...hmmm...what?!,
as we head into the bedroom to disappear
into flesh and bone. Us, the only us. Called.
Mesmerized. Enchanted. Ka-boomed.
Like the man who once won a card game
not by what was in his hand, but the puff
of smoke that was all that was left of him.
You see? We have embraced the thing
of value when we're gone as cloud cover.

Dark So Long We Fear The Light

Marfa sat a beret bottlecap atop her head,
and Big Ek would like to unscrew her fast,
pour Boone right out of her skull. Shaman
of Jeep trails? Him? Seer of the high country
who leveraged the word "snow" to boil blood

in a poem skiers carved into their sticks?
Oh, c'mon! Nature's dead! Heart strings
remain, but it's a guy of 1's and 0's only
that's ultimately in charge of the rain.
Big Ek saw a moose rise on its hind legs

but that doesn't mean fairy tales exist
even if what he saw was actually true.
Snow pack is a thing of lobbyist budgets.
Moose will be the stuff of oatmeal boxes,
something that once was, shot to symbol,

or just mowed down from the everything
of everything tumbling in nuclear freak
storm of weather that's a bunch of guys
deciding it's not worth it to fix it, so
we'll let it ride. Insects can render all

the forests into fuel, till fuel ignites,
and the smoke crosses borders and blame.
Moose are not long for this world. Indian beads,
laughs Big Ek, crackle out Boone's charm?!
But how does Marfa lie with him odd nights

in parking lots outside of poetry readings
where a guy with the gait of old Rambler cars
being pushed to their final service station,
a face hairy as mold, twice recessed, still
strips her naked with mere cadence and promise.

Big Ek once wrote a poem with a last line ending,
"...hologram kiss hologram as simulacra runes."
Boone moaned about a woman's touch—Marfa's?!—
"...healing moon that mountains stretch to reach."
And, "...hands in solar service, light alive."

Right. One thing is a moon and a sun! Oh, c'mon!
It's language that first rose from the muck
"Rock bash turtle. Eat now." Heartbeat rhythm.
Still, none got hugged like Marfa and Boone
at the Cuppa Hope's Wednesday night open mic.

Big Ek once had Marfa to himself, no other
voice so free of dust, stainless steel almost,
some tough chin-first junk, each poem a taunt.
How primal awareness scans all information
for uses, and money is magnetic, in particles

and waves, it moves to be in all one place,
life destroyed from the tsunami of wealth
heading home to the master of this new world,
everywhere the sound of a mirror gutpunched—
nature disintegrates in a rain of brittle cadavers.

Analysis eats data bits, then commands cash.
Dollars send us hanging pricetags everywhere.
Data processing does the rest. Extraction
of all that can be sold, money migration,
until we all agree that digital is better.

The moon is nice, but a computer screen
is where we'll be basking every night!
With no real way to simply shout, "Stop,"
Big Ek gets to work behind a mic stand,
blasting out unembraceable chrome poems

that fail to name a single bush or tree.
"No one wants to recognize their world,"
he told Marfa one night over latte soup.
"Algorithms the new heroin without end."
Hours later, their flesh seemed dated—

sex museum bound—leaving him to wonder
about the coming ecstasy disembodied,
and how long before it's only a matter
of plugging in...hitting the enter button.
Still, that was the end. "Paradigm of fear,"

is what Marfa said, as nicely as she could.
"Write better." They never touched again.
Big Ek saw an empty road ahead that lifted
off of Earth and ribboned into outer space.
The best poems leave you alone. Absolute

of zero. Crumpled can science experiment,
how all the air shoves you inside yourself.
Marfa was the last satellite to receive
Big Ek's signal. To rocket on scared him.
No purpose to discovery without witness.

Poems could never do better than beacon
out to Marfa that one existed as he did.
Marfa and that idiot Boone had a bravery
to believe poetry rewired people somehow.
Big Ek hated faith in an empty universe

in all evidence that nothing changes fast
as he would like it (Big Ek's lifetime!).
Comet's are mostly ice. He sighs a dying
kind of exhaust. Then his skin fell off.
All bullet now. Pure gone. True Big Ek,

destined to cover his own cosmic horizon
in all his unwound string, flattened down
to two dimensions, then maybe beam out
a poet to the Cuppa Hope one day ringing
the stolen truth, as if he was actually there.

Marfa and Boone? "He ain't comin' back.
Big Ek likes people as a concept, but never
in person. Craves the fake clarity of alone."
"And, by the way, we don't rewire folks.
We write for God. In poetry, we pray."

Geometry of Perfect

I guess the rock spoke first,
claiming the waves, stabbed
into the ocean right up front

as if to keep the wild fastened
to the uncomplicated shore.
And kid noises kamikaze against

seagull squawks—kids are chaos,
and a way of counting your years.
Let the chirpy contrapuntal choir

float down the sand, or let me help,
"You want to be by the lifeguard tower!
We don't want those kids to drown!"

I lie on a dangerous stretch of beach
depending on every mother's sense
that no life, no matter how young,

is guaranteed their next breath.
And that white sailboat must be
a message that death will be OK,

at rest, anchored, awaiting, past
the roil of waves, feel of living. My
dead brother's out there fishing now.

And nearly naked women 3, their acres
of skin triangulate me, as sight rolls
up their hills, skis down their slopes,

and I'm happy everywhere I look. You?
Right where you're supposed to be,
staring at me straight through this poem,

as we both create a spirit in the sky.
Information wants to be aware, so flesh
tries to alchemize alphabets to waking.

Mortar, Electrons, Breath & Whispers

Stardust collapses at some point to a nickel thrown
at the change already on the mini-mart counter
next to the pack of donuts and paper cup of coffee.
You say thanks and goodbye and you exit. Outside,
who says a parking lot ain't an afterlife, sneakers
with their own attraction to asphalt, sexy dark hint
of travel? You got a key. You got a car. Whoooosh.
We may be monkeys, but we have fuel, piston, crank.
Soon, you're cloud riding at your work desk, or couch
back home, because none of us really go any place,
and either way, the world God built slips away fast
as grandpa's days, nothing much like the goings on
in little electronic windows, the new where,
cheap little immortals, mugging cash off cameras.

Full cranium dump delivers my own absence of light,
inscrutable stars, lousy scratchjerk amateur's film
that we all build in simple programming rolls
to play our piano in rhapsodies, pastorals, pumping
blues, hysterics, constricting cement, bleak time,
frustrated that our memories are made by only us
and lack the story, the arc, calculus of beauty
in movies played day and night at the multiplex.
Who of us leads a life that could sell popcorn?

Once, I broke down in Tonopah, the open hood
of the Ford called out its puzzle for cousins
and neighbors to crowd me like a desert night sky,
even in silence, they had a different opinion why

the engine don't turn, or I'm the way that I am,
supernovas to dirty spark plugs, we can never
know our location and velocity at once, so there
are no predictions hard safe as a grifter's bet.
I breathe in a jittery universe. Space itself
seems nervous, some reason, the way knowledge
tries to act as if doubt isn't in the kitchen.
Right about the fuel pump, I'm suddenly alone.
The air is thick enough to come from coyotes.
Some of us talk crazy to wonder what we mean;
black hole mystery centers a galaxy of actions.
Bury me alive in the place where this beast dreams.

Wrongly Enchanted We

Apricots

Bombolino dreamed of apricots
the night before he wed. Wondered
briefly the next morning what it meant,
such visitations in our sleep, portent
of a certain kind of sweet, a clue
to look back upon his life as warned
or promised in night's gypsy trance.
Ah, he's fine with chance. The plastic
razor dragged up his outstretched neck,
on a day that unfurled in his head like icing
on a grotesque castle of cake rising
in animation, to flit and fly about. Then,
there, people's voices turned to birdsong,
bright chirping, coo of mourning dove,
everyone everywhere happy and hoping
for the best. How happiness got invented!
Bombolino, all boxed up in a tux, smiled,
and walked some favorite memories to jail

(They knew what they did). A fool no more.
The woman promised to be everything forever,
goddess claim, as if the disappointment
that haunts us all had been eliminated
by vaccine. "We head into the impossible,
I guess," he thought, glad that he still could.
Fearless and stupid is the way to start a family.
Live out the novel, in a book co-authored
by a woman better than he at the life
Bombolino wanted to fill into his old man self.
We end up with the skin of paper bags, and
he wants it jammed with the cacophony
and chaos of kids, days carefully constructed
only to be blown apart again and again.
Stepping from the known universe into another,
the door a strawberry blonde with crooked lips,
eyes animal alert. Every breath needs a reason,
yet even the properties of air may change. No matter,
he trusted the day like the birds and the sea.
Later, his jerk cousin from back East repeats
a line from football days, "You're mortal, man."
Bombolino, certain as the Earth, replies,
"Not today I'm not," grinning like a man
who can't be killed, a man who once walked
straight the path of love, a man determined
to one day plant an apricot tree, and declare
our frontier his. Bloom this desert? "I do."

Pantry

An older man's brain grows a pantry,
around a corner, outside the light,
that creaks in weathered sighs, and lies
draped in weightless drips of dust lace,
stocked with memories separated out
into cans and jars, their labels ghostly.
Only a few still shout "Do Not Touch,"
beneath a cartoon skull and crossbones.
One blows up on occasion from chemicals,
age or climate, and all the stuff inside flows
in sweet and savory syrup across all he knows,
to swiftly disrupt time and mood. Strange
anesthetic feel in every shot of the forgotten.
Other times, the man reaches in and opens
a can of Dad sneaking up behind Mom as she stirs
the spaghetti pot with a wooden spoon, swings
her right around, swoops her low into a dance.
He sings, "Shoofly pie, and apple pan dowdy…"
Now, Mom's gone, Dad stumbles on her name,
and remembering has become an act of faith,
uncertain one can recall the shape of smoke
from a campfire that burned 50 years ago.

In A Cypress Brake — 1981

Little Mama Steele rents out the dock
for catfishing, the juke joint all gone
to bait shop & lunch counter, rickety

as a rich man's speech to God,
the swamp air peeling off the paint,
until the wood aches right out loud,

with brief brittle moans about bones
and the rain and low snakey clouds.
The music's still there somewhere,

so good even Satan gave thanks,
so sad you carried your own grave
home, yes, like the luggage it is.

She still gets tourists, cathedral
shadows on their faces, asking her
if there ever truly was a place

smack where they sat, waiting
on crawfish pie and ghost stories.
"The angel Gabriel and Mr. Scratch,

did you ever really see them here?"
"Yes, at that red table over there.
They'd reminisce on the old days

when they were pals, before man,
before chasing everyone like hounds
to escape the middleground one way

or another," Little Mama teased.
Everyone stops talking for Blind Bob,
and a harmonica solo that could saw

through battleship walls if he chose
to riff an iron ripping frequency.
Bob plays the tourists for tips, but

there was a mission, too. It's all true.
"The people left. Got city jobs,"
he'd say, to explain the now away,

"And, course, back then, wasn't good
to be yourself in these parts. Still,
heroes walked here, in the only joy

outside Church or bed. Happiness,
you know, could get you killed."
On right nights, alone, in delta dark

sliding down wet and thick as jam,
she treats herself to British gin
belts one out again, big blues ray,

unleashing a voice they claimed
could even keep the cops at bay,
or loose the lonesome over to love.

Her eyes latch onto the bye and bye,
a gentleman glows by the fishing rod rack,
panama hat, pearl-handled pistol,

waving her to his red table. Who
enchanted whom? Hard to say back then,
when bullfrogs took the base line

and a wild marsh wind filled in.
Just one generation left still sees
people they know hanging from trees

in the horror corners of fitful sleep, now
all colored by the same bog fog greys
of TV light, as tourists pull into motels

on Highway 61, where clerks whisper
Pinetop, Willie, Sunnyland,
Muddy slept here.

Rectangle

scratch block zen post
speedway freedom old
light kick blam atomic
fragrant last night sold
flag disease peril crest
unleash tits genie love
experiment with reach
sabotage fall next seek
wrongly enchanted we
pearl frost tempest kiss
cranium text birth cave
star jungle death gone
flesh alive cloud rhyme
dream mystery into fire
identity temporal flung
read my prayer rug up
hold on to this bumper

My Devil

You crashed my car, you jerk, and
just after I got the water pump fixed!
You told my boss I wasn't really sick.
Told my girlfriend she needs to know
where we're going, what we're about,
so put me down for a year or two
of hell before I finally get there,
because this sure ain't fair,
to get shoved around, meathooked
onto so many little torments I
can't even enjoy last night's Lakers win.
And who took $20 from my wallet?
Was that you, you son of a bitch?
Whoever you are, wherever you live,
I'll get you for that! You think I'm scared?
Well, I once watched my best friend cry
in a goddamned planetarium light show
because his girlfriend moved to Texas.
And when I looked to see what to say,
there was the desert at night, and stars
shining silent. Just like my idiot pals,
after Mrs. Crockett's funeral mass,
hands in their pockets and nothing
to say either. Somebody needed me,
and I found a Mojave in my chest.
Just so you know, I don't blame you
for that. That one's on my tab. But,
if you would've looked into my eyes
that night, you'd have asked the angels
how do people ever get this sad.

Jar

Type is memory
stored outside the head—
crop for which we're born
—but I prefer this brief flight
remain in you instead,
jam jar of lightning.

Attempting installation:
remember it, and it's real enough
to be harvested
10,000 years from now,
in the resurrection life
of stories told,
retold.

Our deaths fall,
rain upon a sea. Still,
in legend, we will
rise up in wisps...
or waterspouts!

First The Story, Then The Stars, Einstein!

When the night was only black,
flat and desolate as coal dust,

save for a single good luck gnome—
the full moon—a storyteller brash

heard his daughter ask
for something more

upon which to aim her hopes,
than this one soft lamp.

"Firelight in snow!"
"Ah," he said, "First,

"we must spin a tale...
Once upon a time,

"a reckless boy departed
on a dangerous journey,

"down into a deserted mine,
so deep, his devil dared not go!

"Our hero went so far,
beyond all best advice,

"to find cave walls frozen
in blue diamonds beating

"out their own light.
He longed to share

"what lies so deep beneath.
Then, as sudden as desire

"serves as natural law,
this wild herd of sparks

"shattered from the ice,
took flight, and launched

"themselves forever up
into the roof of night!"

The world changes
as everybody sleeps,

and realigns with myth,
so when the next sun

sunk to memory, there
shined the father's gift,

a billion billion ways
for a little girl to wish.

Decorations

My wife stood over this mess
of 200 feet of Christmas lights,

imagined the tangles and knots,
complained of the effort required

to sort everything all out,
until I took the tail of one end

and my wife took the other
in a mad act of small faith.

Slowly we stepped back
until we could see a line

stretched absolutely straight.
Then, we both illuminated.

Download Me Again

We shut down all applications
for a third of every day
to upload and download
the real each night,
our daily agreement taken
from a cosmic server,
with memory, continuity,
and a rigged ending to it all
to better move the story along
—a dream summoning of tomorrow,
with nightmares to threaten breath
and beauty beyond stars,
as a story tells itself into being.

Flesh was invented as a final clock,
then we made it so loneliness kills.

Never was a planet or a sun without us.

Reality is built one day at a time
toward a future that has directed us
because something needs a cloud
of dense memory and best intentions.

When something jams our circuits,
there's the odd poetic moment where
we first know what we didn't know,
but have yet to create the words.

That we seek most we already hold.
There's a crux bud in the cortex
we don't allow to flower.
(We run from it as if seeking!)

It starts plainly enough, the nonsensical,
and we create a world away from it,
all in steadfast agreement…or else, Jack!

Love me doorly.
Guess me on the mouth.
I'm probably you.
Shut down the noisy generals
and simple-minded weaponists!
Ally for peace with all the unspoken.
Download me again.

The Peachful Life

Peach flesh…so good I'd eat peach people.
Send me to a peach church, I'll eat the peacher.
Shaman peach! Tantric peach! Ecstatic peach!
The tongue grows long, wild as a thirsty dog's,
sliding around reckless in full python song
after pink orange bits flung about the cave,
as good gets detonated, the Garden of Eden
emerges in my smile, neurons turn Rockettes.
Why eat books when you can read a peach?
Women await men brained in its peachings.

Famous 2 Poems Shuffled

Dealing cards in a Commerce Casino,
There is nowhere to meet

in service to the ways of luck,
once we've torn out each other's hair

as if a history major wasn't bad enough.
and yanked each other's limbs

Percentages ride the side of loss.
until the joints ache

And you, somewhere, teaching little thugs
out loud, weathered hinges

how to fashion dreams that fit
each failing to consume the other

rather than just taking what they want
still left separate no matter what we did

and selling what's not theirs
too bold and too alike

or what can't be rightly bought.
with the dangerous unique

My La Mirada 2nd floor apartment
lightly holstered, jackets bulging

leans over a rusting, empty pool
ah, if two could be one

decorated in garage sale stuff,
it would have been us

things from grandma's estate.
until of course we'd pull the pin

I blame a tide takes love away.
to blow us apart

Had it once. On a Tate Park bench,
again and again

talking Buddha like a mining project
before the flood of quiet swamps us

or Timewave Zero—cracked egg truth,
ego ever the predator

the deep reveal from drugs or you.
dark matter

Something in me must have caught,
pushes us away

strand of wool in a cartoon sweater,
as galaxies

gone by the time I arrive home.
as we request

You're still out there, a distant shore,
the path of our invention

way to climb out, as a fish grows legs,
fighting singularity as we do

starts to wonder about mountaintops.
for more fun

Can't talk of touch unless I holler
and unavoidable dreams of death

for a choir to come over here at once!
by untoward release

My Theory Of Chance

There was a red dress, silk fireball, cardinal flight,
that stretched and grew at whim...shove of wind,
sudden pirouette, bounce of hips...
with a slight gold trim to sink some greed in.
Legend first born in the mute-calved brain,
which cannot talk but in shadows pantomimed,
so I only sensed it gone from our most lyric bars
and the epic land between curb and cab,
until it autumn leafed into a 10th floor flat
and I followed it to a far corner of the room
across a party sound of crumbling crackers,
people dressed aloud in thin fiction, big purpose,
as if there were no earthquakes
and love had no battle cry.

"I think you wore that red dress to meet me."

"Oh, and what makes you say that?"

"Because here I am."

My Theory Of Time

A red dress in memory before I ever got there,
like blood spilled backstage in the brain slinks
into retinas in all my addiction, gravity, fate.
Hell, I could light a cigarette off that silk!
Longing gets shuffled out of all I keep forgot,
as I deja vu downtown amid bouncing rubber pasts,
to say "hello" to the brittlest caste, waiting to be stacked,
lousy aural fog slick upon my ears as I grab a beer
and turn to see an airy throw of sexfire paint
blot across the room, work of a rebel artist god
to prove we all exist. Rewarded so surrendered,
your red dress calls across amniotic seas,
endless bird flock of years, totem of face
and spell of name.

"I think you wore that red dress to meet me."

"Oh, and what makes you say that?"

"Because here I am." Again.

Indestructo

One arm tattooed with an English garden,
her other sleeved in the gates of Hell,
Len lost the world of Walmarts and dented cars,
diabetes and jerk bosses in that embrace.
Lucky that rich guys think she's crazy,
get scared, and leave her out there
for a guy like Len, with nothing to offer
but his welding skills at Indestructo Fuel Tanks,
and too much time with a pawn shop Fender
played like they were born fraternal twins.
She smokes up, he plugs in, spaghetti strands
of sound riot up the room as the wah-wah blooms
and he sings the new song about her gone
for all last week. She starts to weep. "I won," he thinks.
She builds Len into a granite cliff
that falls to ocean when the guitar's done,
until the night whirlpools above their bed.
"I love my Lanabelle, long may she stray,"
blowing up this ol' worry machine of a world
as she motors from Louisiana to the East Bay,
in her flat-black Merc, red-trimmed rims,
rose deodorizer dangling from the mirror
bold as bait for our baddest no-see-ums.

Postcard From Paris

Kiss sabayon to berries,
butter to warm brioche,
bearnaise to hangar steak,
licks and touches savory to sweet.
Hold each other precious as our only truth!
Art fails us. Politics fail us. People fail us.
All we can do is pray for a bed
in a hotel near the Gare Du Nord
with love savage enough
we win back our souls
before departing
on separate commuter trains
into la vie quotidienne.

Beware The Body Greed

2 ghosts got the body greed
on a gelatinous night loved so
by the deceased. A sick planet
coughs out cigarette smoke
into intermittent fog the spent
color of ash and old dreams
of the wandering dead,
as treacheries come alive.
They spied 2 brothers walking,
short one a banker,
state's best in evictions,
genius who cut the budget
for the bulletproof glass
the head teller begged for.
She was shot just last month
by a man made chicken noises,
as his head leaked the green goo
that lubricates scrape of mind
against the way we all behave
as if a guy could shift an engine
into interstellar space
when he meant to just reverse,
then drive away.
One brother couldn't ever get enough.
"I got some money for you now," said
the banker. "Maybe some next month,
but, Josh, I can't be the government.
I don't operate on luck."
"What do you want, Arn?

A pledge of rough and tough?
I swear to not collapse?
Man, I can't give you that!"
"No. No. Just sign this."
As he pulled an envelope
from his blue suit pocket,
soul doors opened wide
on the despair and distrust,
and both ghosts got a body!
One ghost screamed of mortal rage.
One ghost screamed of mortal rage.

Origin of Ghost Ships

These times fly in locust cloud.
Ate the happiness, man,
right out of my friend's house,
his best memories sunk down
to ravaged stalks, kids unloosed
to the cheapest part of town. They
fight imaginaries from a cardboard fort
in the apartment complex parking lot,
as the family awaits first dead steps
to maybe gypsy bound.
He sends resumes to foreign states
where he doesn't know the freeways yet,
fills out job app forms off paper tablets
at Walmart, Walgreen, Sears,
a nervous fear brining up his blood.
Scratches out errors, draws in arrows,
deep down a canyon with some tourist lost
and yelling for help. Parents stare same
as if he was a wanted man.
Why did he bring all this to them,
like the law was about to come crashing in
for a Dad without a job,
unemployment coming to an end,
waiting for their son to ask for money
like he's pulling out a gun?
Cable long gone, no videos they can rent,
the family inside one lamp, plays Life,
Monopoly, Chutes & Ladders, Sorry.
Or, the parents fight, what the bedroom's for.

Beer. Makeup. Food. School supplies.
This budget scrapes away their skin.
Pantry cabinet reveals their fortunes
in growing expanse of naked wood,
prophecy in spare and dusty prose,
as his wife counts the chili cans.
They moved furniture out at night,
shutting off the front porch light
to stuff the couch into the Astro van
quiet enough to steal it from themselves.
No neighbors to carry their pictures,
end tables, headboards, oak chairs,
like they did when the family first moved in.
Who'd gut a home so cold and quick?
Those fated by HR charts to lose it.
Ghost ship with a residential address,
story for the last school's pancake breakfast.
He stands now where the bitter got born
for all the hard old men he's seen,
salt-cured stance, eyes cemented in,
silent wife, kids who never come around,
words dragged up one bucket at a time.

What We're Born For

Mother worried more the more he grew,
as if the growth might never stop,
and he'd soar straight past Dad,
far beyond his home. A building
might he be at last, she feared,
and all the women it would house,
one yelling, "Wooo-hooo!" out a window
on the 11th floor, "I'm right near the top!"
she yelled to passersby. Mother's neighbors
could overhear, as well as her sister, Jean.
The dirty garages at the bottom,
sound of engines,
where mother just wanted books,
and silence.
A noisy building, all in all,
much too strong, much too tall.
And she hated all its shadow.
All she wanted was a baby in her arms,
and the dreams of how it all would be
Not this.
Not all the space for rent to who knows who.
Not so much city.

His father worried more about the baby and the beast,
how the yapping grows to growls.
What all had God planned
in muscle, teeth and claws,
and how big do you get
when you forget

this is not actually your house?
All he wanted, mostly, was himself,
though nothing near as ornery,
and no one near as big.

The boy grew unavoidably,
as if by nuclear accident.
Got slow mean, tortoise like,
just to have some defense.
He hurt his parents with all his pride,
in peace and tears,
shuffling off their fingertips,
out of dividing cell structure,
and his passion for the long and steady chase.

Apocalips

Render a day from its basic facts.
Squeeze the wet towel, say,
of Tuesday,
and let fall
the movie
you expect
in stills
to the ground.

Get nicely perplexed!
Unembrace your death!
Give feet to dreams.
Let your tastebuds win.
See what you thought you saw.
Take time to velocity.
Find your poles, and spin.
History? Uninvent!
Not so much flesh as rays.
Not so much you,
not so much us,
more like verbs,
so nouns fly off
in startled birds.
Meet me there,
far, far,
unpinned from the flag-
stabbed map
of who we are,
traitorous stuff of stars,

and maybe start anew.
Turn my brown shoes blue.
Comb my hair into a screech.
Kiss tomatoes off divine.

Honey Time

The sun was so much younger then
the waking dawn would yawn out
blues and golds that ran so long
together one day they might marry.

And gravity could not hold me down
the way it does today. I found
my feet in glider shoes, in flight
fast as my forgetfulness of facts.

Teachers bound to get me sure
I was no good, despite applause
from every class at my retorts,
offhand remarks, mutterances.

And you, there, positioned soft
right where I'd ricochet in hard
cracks and smacks upon walls
and desks, football players' fists.

In love with so much, even sadness
in the artist kids, the jumbled crush
of recess blitz, teen eyes of alien
planet satellite disks, I missed

separating you from all of this.
It took me 40 years to see you
standing there, ready to repair
my wrecked chrome wheels,

or slow my piranha flock rush
to eat this life in final meals...
how healing gets concealed
in cotton balls, quiet prayer,

but I hear now how you offered
those to save the frantic boy
from the burden of all that
dreaming, and keep him safe

till he grew the sheer muscle mass
of buildings tall enough to hold
the antenna he'd soon construct
to beacon out unmoneyed truth.

I'm sure you had to learn to judge
and blame to make your way
through all the scheming crowds,
and no one can still believe in me

the way you did back then, but
know I hold you now in honey time,
weep in joy and gratitude to recall
your telling me, "We're fine. Fine."

The Way Ray Lifts Days

Raymond had a mouth could print money, loud
as street repairs when you're trying to sleep in,
bold as a new box of brass bolts. "No big thing
back then. I could lift 30 days. 30 damn days.

Pick 'em up, move 'em. That's a month, man."
Me? Three at my best! Now, each day happens
all over me. Stays right where it started. Dusk
same place as dawn. No one can pick up a day

unless they believe one inch matters. And when
you get this old, each day falls on top of you
in escalator dominoes. Where do I carry a day?
Even if I could get my fingers under it, in full squat,

back straight to lift it safely off the ground, where
do I take it does me any good or helps anyone?
Let's be real. I can't imagine someone lifts a week,
or Raymond once raised a day above his head—

shaking arms, burst apple face, spitting white sparks.
Then, a girl who worked for me in sales didn't show up.
No answer on her home phone. Nothing at her mobile.
Lunch hour, I drove to her condo to knock on the door

or peek in her windows. She saw me, shoved her face
into the crack of the door pressed against the lock chain.
"Sorry" she said in Costco vodka and 7-11 cigarettes.
Disappeared, then finally let me in, releasing the facts

of today all at once like she was pamphleting a town,
as I scrambled up some eggs and started Mr. Coffee.
Eventually, I took her to a Lowe's to buy some paint
and get her bedroom the color she always wanted.

Raised that day right off of her! Know what I mean?
That bum of a boyfriend didn't mean as much. Yes!
I could still lift a day! But, tomorrow's coming down.
Maybe I'll call Ray. How's a man to lift all his days?

Kernel

When we cut the deer apart,
back in Ohio, in full camo,
we shook the old king's antlers
to summon more Miller beer
from the F-150, celebrating
a day we did something right.
The deer had become pests
and the license to kill as many
as our truck could legally carry
served as the start of something
bigger than Monday thru Friday
ever could be, and different
somehow than the Super Bowl
because we pulled the trigger,
we scalped that old granddad,
and we'll always have a photo
of all of us, together, on top,
one foot each on the dead
body of the buck, faces tough.

Then, I got took with the anima,
that old devil religion, spirits
inside every dog, each weed,
like today's sunrise meant a lot,
a world waiting to be hacked
to find who's inside what,
as if I'm a probability and you
are launched the same, but
spun differently somehow,

everything all shot out in dice
on a gambler's boast, velocity
irregular as a corn kernel
on a hot plate—living soil
or lifeless pavement—a sealed
question put to all things,
and we're left to create and
love until we burst in answer.
You can devour all the life
off this rock only to find
we ate our only way to pray.
Doctor and priest both agree
on just how sick and cursed
I am, trying to get exorcised
or medicated out of my head,
while animals jeer, and shoot me
visions of a lone boulder trekking
impossibly across Death Valley.

Blue

blue is the writer's room…
= "how sad"
= "how pretty"
every poem enters a brain
schrodinger's cat
creator and meaning be damned
as language is probability
of blue
in the reader
who believes one can choose
sad from pretty
amid moments dead and alive at once

Unsever & See

It was a bristlecone pine first told me
we have a trigger built into our cells
to disassemble, dissolve into sponge
after so many years, same way the true
knowledge is kept severed from us,
leaving only that washerwoman screech
of a voice inside our heads, scared,
unsure, distrusting, vain, talking a road
scribbled into the Utah desert with a sign,
"10,000 miles to the next stop for gas."
A hoodoo joined in, laughing at our sense
of time, how we got it backwards, unaware
the future fairly demands the best from us,
but we resist. Get a poet in a seance mood,
and he'll tell you how all of our words fail,
as if we invented only tools to stab
ourselves or scrape every living thing
clean off the Earth's surface in a daze
of the most dangerous drugs mistakenly
in our veins just because love is is is
so temporal, and we get so angry.
Listen to a poet out of his mind, and do
what he says to see where you are now.
Yep, that Bryce hike destroyed a man
who grew up wanting to be a cowboy,
have all the promised addictions, and live
as if total control was never in doubt.

One True—Never The Same For 2

The thing between us is a trampoline.
No! Explosions, explosions, explosions...
I'm trying to say: what was never there is.

Once, a man told a story about wheels
and a steam engine, then there was a car
in the thing between us because we listened
to his tales with such wonder.

I met a woman and talked and talked
for years until there was a dining room table
between us and a kid who looked like me
tucked into her arms as she breastfeeds.

Without the thing between us,
we are spheres,
mostly merely near,
and unclear
as anything at all.

No real me
to you, as we are
born again and again
to the thing between us.

The Stuff of Poetry

Angels are more the stuff of poetry
than a garden hose and steel sprinkler fitting,
but 8 minutes of water for the tomato plants every day,
and miracles start to happen on your tongue in six weeks time.
Why is everything not miracle enough?
Identity is the room we build brick by brick
as a way to survive the stories we're forced to tell
in the running tally of who's winning
and who's clearly being tracked by wolves.
But we're all inside every room.
You can tell someone who lost a loved one
that it takes a year to get back to normal,
but language, light as it is, transforms:
"Take one voyage around the sun."

We all know
a bee flies hunched over
as if it's tied by a string to its wings,
but we don't say it.

Denny's - 8:30 a.m., Wednesday

Denny's is not a prison.
It's what I can afford
outside my kitchen cabinets.
The waitress doesn't seem sad
—a low voltage energy powers
her greeting, her scribbles
on the blue order pad,
her twirl and pace back
to lift a dirty plate and place
my ticket up on the drum.
Breakfast is good, and
a broken yolk still talks
of wealth and overwhelming
life. Really, you can't eat better,
at least not in the morning.
I try to hold up my end:
I'm not sad. I remember
the old guys in WWII caps.
I know what they were doing,
as they joked with the girls
and began each story,
"Once, I was back in…"
Turns out old men aren't sad.
We're happy, hopeful,
and slowly saying goodbye
to everything we love.

On a midnight sure next year,
when I've crossed over, come

drink your best Irish whiskey,
all my worst old friends, and
piss free on my pricey grave.

Calamity Divines Clem

Clem's friend Calamity points a dowsing rod
outside her trailer in Free Will, Arizona—named
for the lack of people rather than laws or limits—
at his chest like it found a new magnetic pole.
"No water or underground pipes in here," he says.
Calam's in a denim dress with her hair teased
into some kind of shrub, toy birds hairpinned in
flight around her head, a kid's cartoon scene
of someone just gobsmacked by an iron pan.
300 pounds of voodoo, menace and Jah love,
who moves sexy as island palm trees in funk
harmony with offshore breezes and ukele blues,
red licorice lips wound curious as sex questions.
"I must have slept with 100 boys like you.
Wonder pours from their skin in honey streams,
shoots from their eyes in lighthouse beams,
and I guess one more won't matter much,
seeing as how I do all I can to balance out
this world against the black weight of doubt."
Clem gulped. A noise couldn't be heard
filled up the Sonoran sky, quantum anxiety
of sorts, zinging round in a weather front,
something big seeks to thank him no matter
what he wants. "I never wrote well enough,
Madam Calam. Never earned your bed."
"Hell, man, I prophesy to horned lizards
loud as civil defense sirens every night,
and the future sure comes and goes
much as I announce, but you try to find

a place for that! No. It's guys like you
try to right a whole in this emptiness,
and my answer is to strip, give you
my earthquake of bliss, till you lose
the hospice voice that says give up."
A hand rose, turned, bent. Clem went.
Then the moon came down, and stole
away with the town, much as Calamity
foretold, such as Clem wrought.

Sons of Erin Make Wayward Scientists

Background:
We dig a well with what we believe
then start shoving people in
until the best place on Earth lies
70 feet or more from the real
and everybody down there agrees
on the way things should be.
In this culture of holes, we are
as true as our stories—always
the physics of life among Irish,
where personal history changes
according to the best response
from listeners to any old tale,
because time talking is a gift
of love, and love is the line
in time along which our skulls
slide toward the destination.

Proof:
I had no idea my uncle would rob a bank, or my aunt
would cover for him with a story about Canada and
secret roads across borders when Uncle Roger
was simply cowering under the front porch steps.
But, take the ways to see forever, astronomical tools
big as pyramids, sleek as telescopes and satellites,
and the police with all their radar still can't find
my relatives right beneath their big flat feet!?!

Confirmation:
As old alchemists suggested things as stars,
they found stars. Astronomists theorized
planets just like Earth, and announced
today there's 37 million of them.

Me:
I theorize the brain is a quantum field,
which only begins to explain the Irish.

Egg

Our drummer wanted to get high as the afterllife
most nights, but he pounded out our single heart
with his sticks and skins.
And when I kicked off the red lights
on the first chord of "Panic Town,"
we're lit like hell's house band...
turn every good woman bad.
I'd drive home alone,
but it's like we cored out the night
and we each got a tunnel
of life same as we imagined it.
Then, I'd sit on the couch and wait
for all my molecules to reassemble,
calm down and drink myself to sleep.
All of this, because once I
heard a singer that could shout us
into the neighboring universe,
the place where all our joy
expands us 80 times or more
until you can pull a smile into a field
and happiness finally bursts out and up
as our long wintering primal crop.
Only one out of 180 billion, maybe,
can get through
and fertilize this world
toward its birth.
Yet we all live each day eyes on the egg.
And I play Etta James any night
that seems too small.

Story

We walk around like the planet Saturn
with our story stretching out
as a ring around us
to link with one another.

The terrible thing
is to tell a story
no one believes
or listens to.

Blame language,
and the poet priests,
but life is story.

Tell the story.
Sell the story.
Lie yourself to true.
Revise the story, godlike,
until listeners grow rapt.

Without a story,
you die young.

There is no you,
no flesh any more,
without a story.

I've sat across from people
who didn't buy my story

and I did not exist.

I've sat across from people
who believed my story,
and I was a fable
come real as stars.

A new story,
and we can be more
than what we were
yesterday, how and why
we have time.

Science of Growing Old

The universe swelled again
growing like a family to leave
the first born less and less
until any moment could take

his place, redefine his shadow
as anything important, the new
so cute, so cuddly, so hopeful.
We age into the thing that did its best,

flying to immortal, rocket to the moon,
until creaking bones, recurring cough
and you don't want to know retire us,
destined, too, to dust, like all the rest.

Units of time shrink like dead worms
drying on the sidewalk after the rain.
Soon, time will end, as if it never was,
and here and there just disappears.

We find that death holds no interest,
all the memories in our hands goo
we pull from the bucket and rejoice,
as the wet colors drip from our fingers,

our past, with all the worst forgotten
as best we could. We were once alive.
No need to say aloud that just this
was quite enough. We love astronauts,

the distant planets of which they dream,
and bodies placed on candles built
to explode us past the gravity we share,
the old uncertain that it was ever there.

Litterfall

What I was before the falling leaf:
mongrel chaser of a sudden wind
whooshing through the trees, a hint

all invisible alive that way went,
or maybe a breathless command
in taxis to "Follow that perfume!"

You know what I was...a way
the world could exclamation point,
my warm beating roof above you,

below the pounds of atmosphere.
Wild enough to make rebel women safe,
with a pool hall pose of hustler grace

and the sly summoning of exit signs.
God help me, earth got disappeared
below the concrete and asphalt,

buried dead, nature already extinct
by my teenage years, happy to claw
away at classroom walls, barlight,

interstate horizons, truck cabs,
factory timeclocks, turns 1, 2, 3 & 4
of Central Valley dirt tracks, grey

fabric fencing of the office cubicles,
and all my unstable pals, freedom
their secret love amidst the beard

of recklessness, inattentive at best
to the policies, the rules, the signs.
Decades rolled, ice blocks in a spring river,

and I'm making it clear to a new sales guy
across a satanic cherry wood table,
the room papered in drycleaned faces,

that 2.7% won't cut it any more, man.
Yes, I got enough purchasing power,
where, hell, I could buy my brains out.

But, get me deep into the woods
and I can't tell you what I won.
As I flutter and feather from tree limb

to dank and decomposing forest floor,
an autumn leaf in litterfall, I see
how I turn life obsessively to words,

the way a math professor reduces
all his scenery to numbers,
Yet, I still can't read or speak

to tell you what is happening
in the native language of the world.
I mean, I think I saw the word for torch

in a tree back east one dry, hot fall.
I saw a yellow butterfly surely meant
to punctuate a sentence somewhere.

The Tetons are shouting something out.
The Rockies are Encyclopedia books!
But I was arrogant, I mean, I diagrammed

everything out, only to find you can't
understand a frog splayed across a tabletop
for dissection as much as listening to him talk.

Born knowing what's now a foreign tongue,
with syntax strange enough to have floated
down from Mars, I grew deaf and dumb.

Even time doesn't work as I defined it.
Forever comes in moments you forget
your death, or decide it doesn't matter.

Love is the lightest leash of the Lord.
We hear beneath the avalanche
the calling warmth of sun,

but fail to make our way,
the crush and the cold,
womb and tomb,

is where we choose
to huddle and stay
one more day.

Corsair

With my hips cocked and slanted,
my belt tilted   (slammed damned awry
            as a black restaurant tray
            in the hands of a waitress
            shocked that her ex enters the joint,
            better looking than she remembers,
            with a bimbo neath pink candy hair,
            the hamburgers, fries and Cokes
            sliding off to the plaid carpet below),
I look around for the camera lit red
in this world, and I recall once more
the crystal ball we live in, and see
the seer, the smile and the sneer,
all fingers splayed wide in half surprise
that I would scope the celestial, tear
out my soul, reveal it in light show,
and shout, "I do whatever I want!"
Then strike the moment into print
for you in distance, and your sails,
of which you're mostly hopeful,
until the wind off this strange storm
moves you to realize there is no
weather without will. Sail, reader!
I will never be me, but I'll die well
if I help set the corsairs free
from our meanest, safest harbor.
We'll turn brigand ships to comets,
so the watcher despairs of control
to wonder whose stars these truly are.

Hamlet Days

Inaction piles up, freeway crashes in a death fog.
Voting is a long mangled chain to pull a trigger and kill some kid.

A river of dead bodies, and the neighbors decide
they, too, want to just jump in and float...

live life face down in the diseased water,
breeze on the back their only sense of travel.

Merchants set their hometown ablaze for the money in charcoal.
So much fear that every general gets his own parade.

Hunters and gatherers lock themselves into place. Permanent.
And teach the children food first, then joy, maybe,

until they're dropped in the box truly marked Forever.
Or so, my friend more or less says. He's right.

It's all true. Everything we know is true.
No words exist to argue this.

And, yet, there is a poem.
For no reason at all.

Nothing is the stuff
of our only maybe future.

That's what I try to say.
Tell me I'm wrong. You're right.

We'll Have The Boys Back Home By Christmas

Me, who sifted through the symbols,
gold miner on a creekside, in love
with the facts, breadcrumbs
down the path to the future I chose
from the constant scan of what
means what. Yes, paleo hunter
looking for twig breaks to see
which way the wild boar went...
food for two days, gratitude, pride,
and maybe a moment's rest...
belt buckles, shoes, numbers
on the boarding pass, key fobs,
phones, silver content of a fork,
thinness of the wine glass,
volume of fake wood inside a car,
type on everything from clothes
to billboards, headlines about the same
old shit...Processor! All I know
is we'll be going to war once more
with the best bombs, bullets, toxins
money can buy, as we use up all
the water and soil until the die-off
comes, when we're crushed by clues
of who's sorry, who's next, and why
there are no extraterrestrials.

My Brain Is A Bartender

Each night begins Donner Party beat,
people hungry enough to eat their kin.
Some nights, that's just the way it is,
all our best faded dead away to the one
thing we know we have to have,
communion needed most right now.
No options left. We will fit need
to thing, hole to peg, electron
flow of life despite declarations
bold of our mastery over dogs,
fish, rocks, and, well, everything
else. We're meat and predators,
and they come to me like vampires
in a run on Transylvania's Blood Bank!
I keep them customering...for my tips.
Serve 'em what they want in ways
they can't quite imagine, or ever get
anywhere else just like I make 'em.
Manhattans to margaritas, they come
and come again, so much knowledge
in my fingers, they get thirsty at the sight
of silver shakers, spacecraft in my hands.
They need me to deliver them from all
thoughts of impermanence, and, man,
that crams the tip jar by the register.
You say your life has no meaning?
Well, here! Drink a sloe god fizz!
Your man left you for the waitress
with the Japanese tattoos working

at the Denny's just off the I-5?
Let me pour you a good man will
find you and tonic. On the rocks.
There's this bar. There's the street.
And I deal drinks with no ambition
to truly answer prayers. Call it
a petty crime, but I'm doing life,
so I pay my time the same way
you do. This bar was built here
100,000 years ago, back when
they served honey wine, shroom
urine and masticated ale. Yuck.
They were so goddamned stupid!
Now, I can top off that loneliness
is a mirage martini with a bloom
of lavender flowers! Well stocked
in the storage room, so much so
we've been adding outside units!
Right this minute, I could pour you
what you want for years and years.
Hell, you may beg to live with me.
This bar, the street, the drinks...
One day, though, I hope to stop
the serving. Clear this room out.
Wait and feel...in the epic silence
and love and the holy wholeness,
the entire universe unfold in me.

All The Underworld (Hack The Black!)

we measure life
brief river of light
in the sun and out
cave mouth to cave mouth

trek alert to the dark
for which we're unbred
travel in all weakness
next lies the black

be any age you want
any scary phase
time free
close your eyes

follow the moon
sleep
where you wonder
why you act this way

heart stop
unborn
the lit is for saps
photon addicts

if there wasn't a word
for snow
there'd be no snow
for anyone to see.

Muscle

Silence expanded right to the walls
on our last night, the wreck of two
of us, until I pace an apartment packed
with doughy air, crowded in empty.
I say "Excuse me" as I walk about
to the couch, table, TV chair, while
furniture waits for something to do,
in this movie torn mid-reel, replaced
by a security camera's bleak greys
of a night lobby after office hours,
a place people left to go home.
Spin the infinite in every direction
and no one's there to stop it, so
our radar for each other fails:
where I live is not a location.
Down to my last muscle
against the giving up.
The DJ's voice so chirpy
it must come from the past
on government orders.
My face looks like a word
someone made up.

I know all that's wrong with me.
Whatever's right doesn't take it back.
Yes, I'm sudden. Man, she loved that.
Suddenly, you're in Las Vegas airport.
Suddenly naked on a truck bed.
Suddenly ribeyes follow horse races.

Suddenly, tires wail, "See ya, Mr. Valet!"
Just as suddenly, I guess, I quit
my job. God, I was bored to death.
Arrested for good reason, driving drunk.
Called her Dad a fucking hypocrite.
And, er, ummm, tried to lose her cat.

Mad love can't handle half of anyone
young, so we decide to age, yes, grey.
I'll simmer down. She'll accept less.
I hope she finds a better man than me.
And when I call years from now—I will—
I hope she's happy enough to say no.

Next, the night crushes down so hard
I can shove my arm into the stars.

Dawn of Gone

Old man winter hit me up for cash
I gave him a stick

blaming him for the lack of green
He blames the same on me

"Our one true poverty is time"
Points to the muddy ground

"Right there I wrote my name"
I know just what he means

life on a visa
We are known briefly

in the season of here...me
and all the big bang-boom

alive and shuddering youth
wonder sparked to overload

until a whip and a chair
comes to you with age

The big men get to boast
"Once I was a blizzard..."

We swap stories about storms
and how summer's not for us

when our kids will have kids
as they summon their sun

I guess I'll go where winter is
I ask him what he knows of this

"We go to the other side, my friend
And with the urging of that light

those buds, who are we to stay?"
The greatest beauty is goodbye

In the dawn of gone, all
our memories are now

Croc

California summer days enter winter bright
as angels into rooms full of purgatory.
Stuffed deep as a bad feeling into the third floor,
my head submerged below cubicle sightlines
in a grey fabric fog color of horror film sets
when the creature roams a vague netherworld
and villagers disappear in a cloud center of revenge,
grey as the 'good job' narrative, grey as sidewalks,
a grey injected into the vein each paycheck.
But I am no dead log in the negotiated river,
having climbed so many walls of experience!
My eyeballs once ricocheted off a ceiling
loud and clickety clack as ping pong balls
from the way she did the Louisiana python thing.
Rode an astral drug elevator one Tucson night
straight to Reno and back so real I phoned the casino
to request the winnings I left in the sports book bar.
Drove a rental car straight into the ocean at Daytona.
And maybe Cathy's got a mystery mass in her breast,
Elaine's sister is chasing a soldier to the coast,
Robert will get fired for sleeping with the woman
one floor below (fire, moon and star tattoos!),
but it remains the stuff of Tigres/Euphrates Rivers
10,000 years back when we first sat still as this,
when all adventure stopped and we waited
on clouds, on approval, on luck, on storage
(farmers, office workers eat the same dust).
No more! I'm the guy who rid identity
to free up awareness, the guy who shut off

the lying, treacherous snake king voice,
skull emptied of its rabble...my quantum field
in a bone temple, organic mass draped off it,
opening the processor to neglected info
so that I may one day stop the world
(vision that sees past movie screens).
You hear the same story a million times,
and, c'mon, man, all meaning ends.
More stories about bags of meat?!?
I am not me, nor ever have been.
Slip to pure listen to escape thought:
computer fan, office weather machine,
electric thrum, gurgle of computer keys,
Robert whispers junk, the light unaware
this old buried thing is coming for it.

Once, I Was

Disease of another type begins in the waiting room
with a TV locked on an autoimmune disorder channel:
white-haired woman explains it's not so bad,
but you do have to give up cross-stitching, and
find other things to love. TV or soup or walks.
You always pay your deductible right away,
then wait 45 minutes for the doctor.
He needs tests first of all, so it's two weeks
of blood work, MRI scan, results allowed
only for him to see because who are you?
In the meantime, heavy doses of drugs
that are poisonous over the longterm, so
it's only temporary, until a regimen, also
poisonous enough to make you sick
each week, thin your hair, who knows
what else, called chemo pills, that work
only so well, unable to fix a finger, knuckle,
two knee caps, leg cramps, chest aches,
and you can only recall the old lady on TV
gently guiding you on how to give up.
You also wonder why they don't drill
a hole in your head, let the demons out.
The ear doctor explains, "You're going
to have lifestyle changes. They start
with turning the volume of the TV up."
But you've aged out of any rights
to complain. Lucky to be alive. Yes,
true enough. Illness is the creak
of the door closing slowly. Once,

though, you served as an eye of God,
as He worked to figure out what is
dream, what's actually happening.

Calling All Copters

My history floods old streets
until I need a boat to get around.
But, there's still the sound
that once was rumor,
now loud as a waterfall
roaring out in hunger
as if it smells me. Yes,
the water keeps rising.

Yet, what I fear most
is a clear day,
hard desert noon
that hunts all moisture,
zaps it and evaporates it,
until the world is stopped,
and my town's gone.
What's left is beyond
our little bricks of words,
and so nothing can be built.
No houses, no avenues, no asphalt.
Extravagantly empty. Impossible.
Left alone on the rock long sought,
Philosopher's Stone. I lack the guts
for anything but nails, 2x4s, hammer,
saw, construction and collapse.

Yes, we're dying. Yes,
our skin falls toward the floor,
weathered at the same pace

as a backyard fence.
Yes, we'll be no more.
But what scares us most
is ever the sacred Now,
moment we could choose
the loneliness and wonder
of being transformed, not
rescued from the rooftops.

Calling all copters:
When the clock's straight up,
this whole house is gone.

Down The Hall

I see her a lot at the end of a hall
wallpapered alive at her end
in leaves that turn constantly
to seek out the missing sun.
The light shines from her skin,
as she moves in control
and abandon at once,
muscled and liquid as green
life waffling gently in a wind,
sorting through each breeze
for economy, grace, art, fuel,
in the pointy shoes of a jinn.
She disappears only if I step
toward her, so the darkness
of the corridor can never be
traversed, bulb light to sylvan,
except, perhaps, upon my death.
Often, now, her hair is grey,
color of volcanic ash, burnt rock,
and lays wiry alongside cheeks
drawn in and lined, beneath
shadow eyes, in a show
of great age, in kind regard
for my advancing state.
My old mystery friend.
Might as well try to rope her
as write about her. Skittish
as any other wild animal,
knowing so well what men do.

Carlotta, Mist & Rain

Mist mills through a granite valley,
vaporous grey sheep colliding to stone,
sky electrocuted into a cobalt plane
head high above Sierra peaks.
No, you should never hike alone.
Carlotta.

They must have sent an archangel
because this one in the dream was angry,
said he was going to make me eat my sins.
Then, he started shoving coal into my mouth,
which I just chomped on and swallowed
until his hands were black and empty.
I smiled.
"Didn't your sins make you sick?" he asked.
"Man, I was raised on fear. Makes sin taste like
vegetables."
Carlotta.

Well, sir, I didn't believe the morning sun
would take away the night, unless
my dark grove said so.
Carlotta.

Antidote for men
who believe in such a thing as choice,
her curves best presented on NASA telescopes
to take us back to where it all begins.
Carlotta.

The rain parachutes down in little strangers
to a city that doesn't believe in climate.
A grey day in LA is a do-over,
clearly someone's mistake,
or a steady pelting of reminders.
Carlotta.

She once grabbed a bag of charcoal
at the carniceria to cook up the carne asada
for her father's birthday. I hesitated.
"It won't rain."
Oh, Carlotta.

Turtle

Just another midnight, common.
The ice maker breaks loose
a rattling toss of bones noise,
sound of Golgotha gamblers,

to add unease after a leaden day,
all color collapsed to hardening
cement, sky of sludge and guilt,
no one awake but a greying man

who may sit and watch TV,
or think again of throwing it all away
to begin anew. Eyes closed, ah sure,
he gives the dark its complete run

from outside his head through
to outside again, leaving him
wondering if the dark out there
thinks like the dark in him.

We wait around to prove our fear,
it seems, just like that dream awake
he had years back of a witch
never quite seen,

just a dying cat voice
from a jagged shadow
out past his window,
beneath a wavering moon

and a live oak tree. Unbeknownst,
she needed in, to cook the happiness
that coursed through his house then,
as his wife and kids slept. Family life,

he feared, was built on deceit. Yes,
they felt safe now, but he knew nights
are crowded with predators in flesh
and invitation. He stood at the window.

At the window, he stayed. Braced
for the curse that might come. Dawn,
he startles awake in stuttering breaths,
and glories in his long run of legs,

thrust of arms and hands before his face.
Alive, unchanged. He kept that night
refrigerated so fresh, it comes to him still
to take a bite. He had protected them.

Scrawny neck, little bald head,
hard shell a man's life builds…
he wonders yet, if the witch, in anger,
had cast some spell no kiss could fix.

As he reminisced— he always did
when the drinking's done—he pulled
the recliner's lever to deep sleep.
O, how close he'd come to fable.

Who We Are Now

In praise of futures born in daydream,
glints of sun off taillight chrome, willed,
until our old problem with here and gone:
life marches, man, undrilled, on and on.

Awareness comes one person at a time,
most incapable of seeing any signs, or
reading any runes to open up the night
into which we spark the dawn each day,

while we curse the physical world
for outliving us in rock, sky
and water, leaving us cousin
to brief fire as if it had memory.

Untrained today to hear voices
from beyond, in old guidance,
or glide along our fate easy
as floating down a slow river,

we rush to distraction, spend
time as slot machine coinage,
and silence receiver drumskins
with cheapest, dullest drugs.

An old man starts over. All
is only because he sees it,
eyesight a wizard's wand,
the summoner...creator.

He codes a new faith, a sea
from which we rise, crash
and return to ocean. Simple.
We will ourselves to surfer,

and talk and talk the next day
into waves, where we stand,
fall, head back out for more,
in wolf balance, adrenal flow.

As he walks out the front door,
it is his world, at last the alone
he had feared so long. "Mine!"
O, the distance of loved ones!

It is his responsibility to see
the drought trees, smoking VW
of the neighbor kid, the dead
lawn next door as it tells a tale

of his alcoholic friend. Brick houses
and black driveways arise empty
of meaning, until vision delivers up
a hummingbird. "Yes. That's it."

But he wanted to say, "That's me!"
He wanted to shout, "I did that!" Soon,
with every step, he allowed another square
of pavement in the sidewalk just ahead.

Dylan

a young man once sang out
as if his blood could fountain but he would not die
fearless, with flesh shining like movie screens
and animal documentaries flashed across his face
arms upraised in a V shape as if designed by Tesla
destined for electric coils to spurt and sputter
above his head uplifted because the sky talks
as he opened his mouth and tried to shout
rejoice
in a way
that drilled him by his soul into the ground
and astronomers on other planets saw
hope
and hurried away from their telescopes
to tell their kids, their wives, their mothers,
their brothers and, hardest of all,
fathers
the finest prayer we ever heard
steady pulse of anger in a guitar strum
makes us hesitate in the witching hour
along a line of streetlights in a night fog
we follow as our only truth
until we stop, light a cigarette
and linger
in wonder
at every song's demand we
join him where
the river flows

Pond

Meteor snaps to flame. A bird
turns its head unaware—sense
of dread as true as hunger.
Its bones, its ashes, then ride
the wrong side of a shooting star
to the ancient target of our ground.
No escape from the errant velocity

of everything, the way Richard C.
drank all that hero juice and drove
his Dad's Camaro straight to redline.
The crash took forever. Street lights folded
into old and droopy orchids (all color gone),
the crumpling metal sounded planned,
with the station wagon big as a drive-in screen
for his last movie. Another doomed mother
shouts her kids' names so they'd hear
how sorry we can suddenly be.

A grandson announces all he's going to do,
and Grandpa says, "All there is for any man
is to accept himself before he's gone for good."

Members of the day's Kiwadi Wash patrol
whisper code into headsets to take their positions
while the mujahedin gesture to each other silently
for everyone to find the best rock they could,
and the firing started, with America's best
M4 Carbine Assault Rifles, designed by Colt,

5.6 millimeter caliber bullets, gas-operated,
firing off 700 to 850 rounds per minute,
while 7,000 miles to Washington D.C.
a technician on satellite duty jokes,
"Man, that's miles and miles of nothing."

Back in L.A., Officer Hickman worries
about his Hazmat suit, and the holes
it's getting from all the use, budget cutbacks
in the way of safety, while the highways amaze
with the volume of better and better poison
getting trucked to U.S. farms and factories.

Florida panther wears the night
like Dracula's finest emperor cloak.

Mojave rattlesnake glories on a pocket mouse
and the feeling he won't have to eat for a week.

California condor plummets in ragged shadows
after drinking from a puddle of antifreeze
left over from a radiator flush outside Fillmore.

Johnny Bongos comes in from a cigarette,
announces if the jungle wrote a book,
most people'd be dead before they finished it.

And as much as Rita loves the little drunk,
her debt to trouble's long paid off, and
in a world not built for saving poets,
what's a dreamy sales admin to do,

with Johnny seeking the same destruction
killed his father, as if knighthood waited.

A crane follows the interiors of its DNA south
over New Mexico, but that old pond is gone,
wings turn to solid wood, then air fails.

Ta-Pocketa

What if God gave me the sky
and let me write upon it
in letters two clouds high
so a line of poetry stretched
halfway across the state?
Yes, that's when I'd learn
I've nothing much to say.

But, wait! I've got this engine room,
I'm sure, somewhere in this skin,
with a door I go through time and again
into steaming, grimy, ta-pocketa space
that grew to power my place in this world,
unnerved bosses and made contractors do
exactly what I said and for how much,
made women take inventory for the man
they'd someday hope to get, kept
mechanics and car dealers fairly honest,
fixed broken things in single Saturdays,
paid all the bills even in the broke years,
so a wife and kids could believe me
when I said, "It's going to be alright."

I'm going to waste the sky for that?

Let's save the sky for all
its hellos and goodbyes.

L.A. Apocalypse Cartoon

The heat cooked Thursday to 98 degrees,
a November record for a city that advertises
weather to the Midwest and Back East,
while it rings up its fattest paychecks
infecting China with Hollywood outbreaks.
Adam tried to talk to his girlfriend again
about moving to where there'll be water
10 years from the day he might propose
a life together. "So, let's go there, and
make plans in one last atmosphere
similar to where we grew up. The temp
of California left long ago for Oregon.
When we die, Malibu will be way up,
in some beachtown near Anchorage."
Candy just got her Japanese tattoo
declaring her faith all will be OK. See,
inside her, a new doomsday scene
arrives every day. Earthquakes tear
apart the city stone by stone, ground
rising to meet rooftops falling down.
Righteous riots. White devils. Disease.
She smokes a joint to glue it all back.
"I can't relocate like we're refugees,
babe. It's bad mojo. It's giving in.
We must live what we believe,
and we can't let our lives be sold
out from under us, for final profits
in banks without tellers or guards,
just strings of code on the internet!"

Adam wanted to say 200 years
is all that history's got left, and
we'll be lucky to be dead, if we can
still die on time 50 years from now.
"Eugene will be good for us.
We're a day's drive from friends
who'll stay here with no choices
left but to beg one day to live
with us, where there's still water."
Candy swore to keep her L.A.
cell phone number always, forever,
as if she once lived in Atlantis.

The Phantasm Quartet (And Who Are You?)

1)
People live with a spirit hat,
only once removed:
in line to heaven's gate,
so the dead can discover
the single thing they collected
all their lives, every day, stuffed
into the cap, fedora, beanie, beret,
or big and bouncy thing with wings and lace.
The dead are puzzled at what they'd done.
One person dofts a hatful of snowflakes.
Another a hatful of post-it notes.
Pocket knives, flower petals, rocks
shaped like hearts, diner matchbooks,
beer bottle caps, old pencils, good pens,
ATM receipts, funeral cards, shiny pennies....
the dead joke about being so unaware.
Each night the angels talk as they unwind;
again one asks, "What was the point of that?"
Some say man suffers so from language.

2)
His name was more an address,
his body a building, its architecture
long out of favor, with tenants
in the hundreds, his brain serving
as an exhausted landlord, tired
of all the yelling, loud parties,
sad stories when the rent's due,

evictions, and those gone missing.
Once more, he hears a knocking
at the door, and he mumbles loud
as a troll beneath a wooden bridge,
schoolchildren running just above,
"Ahhh, shurrruppp." His keys
rattle now like chains. He dreams
of a day he hands them over,
and walks namelessly away.

3)
Plane bound for Orlando, my new hell.
He falls hard into the seat next to me,
a guy in a suit you buy 2 at a time
on a promise of delivery in 3 days,
drunk upon boarding, ready to talk,
and I hate revelation. God shock
after leveling off at 32,000 feet:
"That song, Vous Deux Love,
I wrote it, I sang it, I sold it!"
The radio had been my only map
out of my hometown, and, holy shit,
this was Mark LeFevre of Bango!
I summoned that song to appear
on an AM station one summer
in prayers answered hourly!
"It's more beautiful than me,
man, it still makes women fall;
it still makes people wonder about
whatever they can't figure out, man."
OK, I hated him for being old,

the puffy, sagging skin, and hair
hanging like dead ferns off
a grey, pink, yellow cliffside.
He sells portable spas now
for Dad's above-ground pool biz.
"That's just the way it is, man.
I shrivel, and will die one day, but
the song sails out forever, if
done right, to unknowable code."
He wouldn't shut up. Wrecked
my old teenage source of power
fast as if I'd found Mom paid
Darlene Adams for my first kiss.
"We die. The nothingness of song
lives, man. We cast the spell!"
When he said we're all just sacks
of swamp water, I ordered drinks
so he'd fall asleep and I could finish
my PowerPoint presentation...
marching orders from the boss:
"Dazzle 'em . . . or else!"

4)
Born pregnant, we all carry
the secret, slippery thing, held
in a balloon, stuffed somewhere
behind the ribs, inside the stomach,
inside entrails. Or it wanders
around as we walk into the bar
to a new place as we stagger out.
Yet we know nothing of its birth,

shocked one day to ache of gone,
with no evidence in the world
the missing child was ever born,
had ever lived, had unfurled
in action and color against
this still world that still exists.

Flash

i ran until i reached the speed i knew i could become
ran right out of clothes
clean out of skin
straight past my thoughts
my name
my sense of sorry for all the stupid things i've done
history exploded like the barrier it's always been
JFK went one way, my mother the other
as if time was never truly a line of any kind
just a throw slow into the air of softly packed snow
too quick to hear anyone's response to anything I said
too fast for dead
sheared from any need to wait
universed around
so lonely bound
mothers warn their children
not to race so hard
against the light

Dream Of Mass

A night breeze slithers around your neck,
your waist, a snake, python that ropes
you into its grip, until what you are is the place
someone waves goodbye to from their car,
as if you were dressed in old front porch,
gravel driveway and aluminum siding.
Your last map is something someone said
once
about a hilltop
in a distant city,
a neighborhood that began with what can
percolate and bubble up through manholes,
the old ways, the demands of earth for us
to go on and connect it somehow to sky,
as if we were lightning bolts, horizon lines.
We cannot be anything but the hope that
escape colludes with will, impossible, yes,
in such a way to make something, finally,
akin to brick and mortar, and not song
or laughter or story, cursed as we are
by a sprinkle of time. Ineluctable mass!
We look for something that can be put
in a pocket, and kept in a drawer,
long after we're gone, buzzing,
hissing, sparking, smoking.
And we'll yell from the other side
what to do with it, but only
small children will hear, and
they, too, are told not to go near it.

Small Proof There's Only One Of Me
(plasticized and in my wallet)

when the glaciers all run backwards to their coffin in the
        glen
and seismic is the weather, unknown today's forecast
when lions get that rag doll look, the suburbs hear hyenas
        laugh
and elephants grow tired of hiding bones of their deceased
when the bankers kill their children, then beg pity from the
        crowd
corporations tell their congressmen to vote us all hellbound
and prisons grow until they're visible from outer space
when the ocean refuses borders in its shores, rain burns up
        the crops,
the sun demands we tithe in sweat, rivers blow right
        through the dams
when God says, "I told you so," and the other gods agree
poets write and rewrite wills, lawyers bill us for their tears
teachers tell the classroom clown, "Go on, this time is
        yours"
when the only thing that matters is one last kiss
close your eyes and remember this

Outside

An old man will say, of course,
the ocean was never the ocean
when you were 10 years old,
shivering, determined that summer
to throw your body with the waves
the way the older boys did.

Ocean tries to eat everyone,
but the boys laughed, looked ahead,
and sung themselves along a curl
of water that had no need for them,
and you'd always see their heads
pop back up in wondrous signal
that they lived again and again.

There was dishwater inbetween,
the big waste of time and space,
before the perfect taking-off place,
blue and rising and urgent as last
words before a nervous firing squad.

In a quick quiet, you cross the grey
water of purposelessness. Back
on the sand is the life you may not see
again...going on fine without you.

Just bobbing. Wobbly afloat. Feet far
off the bottom. Wondering. Someone
says cooly, "Outside." They head on

to meet it. You go. The monster comes.
You swim hard into its wings, its flight,
until you're staring down a building.

And my life was only my life,
with not much left to it now.
"Outside," of course, was never
a word. It's the gong that made me,
maybe, eternal as some dawns.

www.ingramcontent.com/pod-product-compliance
Lightning Source LLC
Chambersburg PA
CBHW071312110426
42743CB00042B/1279